Nature's Domain
Anne Lister and the Landscape of Desire

Jill Liddington

Pennine Pens
www.penninepens.co.uk

First published 2003
This edition 2019
eBook edition 2019

Pennine Pens
www.penninepens.co.uk

In memory of
Elaine Connell
1953 - 2007
co-founder of Pennine Pens.

Contents

List of Illustrations

1. **Cover**: Anne Lister portrait
   By kind permission of Calderdale Museums

2. Shibden Hall, by John Horner, Buildings in the Town & Parish of Halifax, drawn from Nature, 1835. Page 9

3. Anne Lister's diary page: 16-8 May 1832
   By kind permission of West Yorkshire Archive Service, Calderdale. Page 27

4. Ground floor plan, Shibden Hall (as it might have been in 1832) (based upon *Shibden Hall, Halifax: a visitor's guide*, 1998). By kind permission of Calderdale Museums. Page 42

5. Map of Halifax, Shibden & Lightcliffe. Based on Myers' Map of the Parish of Halifax 1834-35. Page 53

6. Map of Shibden Hall Estate belonging to Mr James Lister, 1791 SH:2/M/2/1/2/2 (part of) .By kind permission of West Yorkshire Archive Service, Calderdale. Page 54

7. a) Forms of Prayers for the Use of Christian Families, Rev Samuel Knight, Whitley, Halifax 1829. By kind permission of Calderdale Library and Information Services. Page 96

8. b) Letter, Ann Walker to Anne Lister, 24 Dec 1832, SH:7/ML/ 644/1. By kind permission of West Yorkshire Archive Service, Calderdale. Page 109

Preface to 2019 edition:
Anne Lister sixteen years on

Carefully re-reading the pages I wrote sixteen years ago, I'm delighted to discover that very little needs correcting or updating. The sense I made then of Anne Lister's diaries still stands. So I've preserved the text of the 2003 edition, correcting just a few minor errors that had somehow crept in.

Nature's Domain builds on the work I'd done five years earlier, for *Female Fortune: the Anne Lister diaries 1833-36* (Rivers Oram Press, 1998). One of the book reviews was headlined: 'She was butch, "married" an heiress and ran her own business. Oh, and it was 1835'. More thoughtfully, another reviewer, asked:

'How did she get away with it?... Above all it was her total and uncompromising rejection of heterosexual marriage that sustained her... There was just no language with which people, whatever they felt, could attack her... As Liddington acutely puts it, Anne Lister's identity was defined in the eyes of others by class, land-ownership, dynasty and education, not by a sexuality (whose name) had not yet been invented'.

Such reviews made me go back earlier - to 1832 when Anne Lister returned home to Shibden from her travels. Like *Female Fortune*, for *Nature's Domain* I determined to read - and present - Anne Lister's diary *just* as she wrote it. For each day, even each hour, handwritten & coded sections intermingle intimately. These magical juxtapositions of public and private cannot be wished away. Some enthusiasts plunge straight into the coded passages - and stay there, reading the handwritten sections rather as an afterthought. Heading to the coded passages is of course highly enticing. But, as the reviewer quoted above states, it is only by grasping her social class, a member of the minor landed gentry, that we understand 'how she got away with it all?'

*

So here I dig deep - to see how in 1832 Anne Lister came into her own. Many readers' first encounter her through Helena Whitbread's *I Know My Own Heart* (1988) which mainly focuses on the coded sections of the earlier Anne Lister (1817-24). But this young woman was not the mature and powerful Anne Lister 1832.

So what does *Nature's Domain* tell us? As the 2003 Introduction states, it tells us that Anne Lister returned home despondent & empty-handed, betrayed by yet another woman's marriage plans. That she soon determined to reinvent herself. No longer traveller and high-society flirt, she would remodel herself into the commanding owner of Shibden's ancient acres. She elbowed her old-soldier father and irritating sister Marian out of the way. And, like any other member of the landed gentry, she would seek a companion for life. And all this remodelling was *urgent*!

Jane Austen's *Pride and Prejudice* was published in 1813. Two decades later, Anne Lister could well have subtly adapted its unforgettable opening: 'It is a truth universally acknowledged that a single woman in need of a good fortune must be in want of a wife'.

So *Nature's Domain* tells of Anne Lister's wooing and seducing neighbouring heiress Ann Walker - a courtship conducted in the conveniently intimate female space of the moss hut Anne Lister had built in rural Shibden, conveniently away from relatives' prying eyes.

Anne Lister was ruthlessly adept at manipulating a truth and then re-presenting it to her own advantage. Recipients included not only isolated lonely Ann Walker, but also a wider cast of characters. Her younger sister stood little chance: by verbal manipulation, Marian was soon in thrall to Anne. And, come the December General Election, Anne Lister - by now a staunch true 'Blue' - had no qualms about coercing her enfranchised tenants into voting Tory. Women (even land-owning women like Anne) might not have the vote. But that mattered little with no secret ballot yet. She'd know *exactly* how her tenants voted.

*

By the time *Nature's Domain* came out in 2003, I'd worked intensively on Anne Lister for about fifteen years: I needed a break. And I was drawn back into Votes for Women. *Rebel Girls* (Virago, 2006) told the Yorkshire suffrage story.

However, in 2010, I took a holiday from Votes for Women, pulled back into Anne Lister's world by the BBC2 drama starring Maxine Peake. And being filmed for the accompanying documentary, presented by Sue Perkins. Then in 2011, the Anne Lister diaries were added by UNESCO to the UK Memory of the World Register - documents of especial cultural significance. Global recognition indeed!

More years passed. I remained committed to Votes for Women, and *Vanishing for the Vote* (MUP 2014) presented the suffragette boycott of the 1911 census.

*

Time passed. Since our earlier Anne Lister work together, I'd almost lost touch with scriptwriter Sally Wainwright. (See 2003 Preface.) While I had revisited suffrage history, Sally was producing award-winning tv drama series: from *Scott and Bailey*, to *Last Tango in Halifax* and *Happy Valley*.

But Sally's fascination with Anne Lister never left her. And in 2014, I was both surprised and delighted when on *Desert Island Discs* Sally chose *Female Fortune* as the book she'd like to take away with. Indeed, Sally was soon back writing scripts for her Anne Lister drama, the first episode opening on Anne's return to Shibden in May 1832. And I returned to my role of historical consultant.

However, Vote 100 suffrage celebrations soon loomed. So I was drawn into working on Votes for Women 2017-18, and others took over the consultants' role.

*

Now, finally, in 2019, Sally's BBC1 drama series *Gentleman Jack* is ready. Series 1 is inspired by both *Female Fortune* and *Nature's Domain*. Anne Lister is played by Suranne Jones who starred in *Scott and Bailey*. With HBO media publicity plus UNESCO cultural recognition, Anne Lister's reach will now surely be global.

*

So, it's time to reflect back over these sixteen years. To look from *now* to *then*.

First, what new do we know about Anne Lister? Two scholarly works particularly merit noting. The first, an admirable PhD on *Moving between Worlds: Gender, Class, Politics, Sexuality and Women's Networks in the Diaries of Anne Lister 1830-40* (1995) by Cat Euler of Arizona University, is now available online. Second, Alan Bray's *The Friend* (Chicago University Press, 2003) persuasively sets staunch Anglican lesbian Anne Lister in her traditionalist religious context.

More recently, there have more popular books too. The biography of Anne Lister by German LGBT writer Angela Steidele, *Gentleman Jack: Regency Landowner, Seducer & Secret Diarist* (2018), has the distinct advantage of compressing Anne Lister's millions of words within one volume. However, discerning readers will quickly grasp that Steidele has not herself read the diaries, but has borrowed heavily and wholesale from Helena Whitbread and myself. Likewise, I've been alerted that the story of the Ann Walker courtship and seduction I tell in *Nature's Domain* has already been turned into a chick-lit novel....

*

At the time, back in 2003, I hadn't fully appreciated how this 1832 section of the diaries (just 8½ months) was in many ways the crucial missing link - between Anne's past and Anne's future. It was the time she determined to remodel herself. It was when she came into her own, as the imposing inheritor of Shibden's ancient acres - albeit one 'in need of a good fortune and in want of a wife'. Anne Lister wanted power - not just over Ann Walker but across her world. The compelling dynamic of these 1832 months provides the hook on which hangs the first series of *Gentleman Jack*.

Jill Liddington, March 2019

Shibden Hall, by John Horner

Buildings in the Town & Parish of Halifax,
drawn from Nature, 1835

Preface to 2003 edition and Acknowledgements

I grew intrigued by the Anne Lister diaries for 1832 about twelve years ago when I started reading and transcribing some of these pages. I returned to them again in 1996, and then for a third time in 2002-3. So along the way, there are many people whose help I greatly appreciated.

First, I would like to thank West Yorkshire Archives Service (WYAS), Calderdale, where the original Anne Lister diaries are preserved as part of the much larger Shibden Hall papers: in particular, Principle District Archivist, Pat Sewell, plus Ian Thomas.

Helena Whitbread, whose 1988 book initially sparked my enthusiasm for going back to the original diaries, has since then generously shared her encyclopaedic biographical knowledge of Anne and her lesbian relationships.

Polly Salter, Museums Officer for Calderdale's Social History Collections, joined my 'Anne Lister: Reading her Writing' course at Shibden Hall, and wrote on Anne and science; and the other staff at the museum, particularly Val Stansfield and Tony Sharpe; also Rosie Crook and Barry Sheridan of Calderdale Museums and Arts.

So why have I gone back to late 1832 for a third time? I kept thinking I could put Anne Lister, and certainly these few months, right behind me. But recently I have been summoned back – largely by growing public interest in Anne Lister.

*

Initially, this came from WYAS's digitisation project, funded by the New Opportunities Fund. The 'Yorkshire Women's Lives On-line' project engaged Helena Whitbread and myself to select and transcribe 60,000 words for its website – and I decided to include three long passages from late 1832. I would like to thank to Ruth Sharpe, project coordinator, plus Sylvia Thomas and Keith Sweetmore of WYAS who have ensured that the journals reach a far wider public readership.

Then in summer 2001 I met scriptwriter Sally Wainwright, who wanted to portray the Anne Lister of the mid-1830s. Many, many emails later, Sally has skilfully distilled the essence of the story into a film treatment. As we walked round Shibden in the rain, it was Sally's enthusiasm and perceptive questions ('So where was Anne Lister's moss hut?') and the very real challenge of relying on unpublished transcripts, that persuaded me, once again, to turn back to the late 1832 diaries.

Alongside this, I was approached about a programme on the history of homosexuality for the *Georgian Underworld* Channel 4 series, and again I found myself going back to the 1832 pages; and so thanks to Jo Evans and Neil Crosbie for filming in unheated Shibden Hall on the coldest day last January.

All three projects persuaded me during 2002 of the need to go back to these eight and a half crucial months, to look again at my old 1991 shiny dark-grey-on-light-grey microfilm-reader printouts of 1832, to revisit my early stumbling attempts to make some sense of Anne Lister's richly diverse daily life then, and to ensure more systematic transcription and publication (so that hopefully there would be less need for argument about what Anne *was* doing then).

Finally, many thanks to Chris Ratcliffe at Pennine Pens for taking on Anne Lister – again. Chris's superb technical skills meant that the complex manuscript was handled with great efficiency and speed. For very helpful comments on an early draft, I am most grateful to Helena Whitbread, Polly Salter, Angie Cairns and Alexandra Mathie, Ruth Sharpe, Sally Wainwright, Elaine Connell of Pennine Pens, and Julian Harber. Also, to Angie Cairns for expert copy editing; to Tim Atkinson for discussion of 1830s' geology; to Alan Petford for photographing the 1791 map; and my special thanks to Julian for horticultural information, for willingly sharing our house with Anne Lister for so many years, and for walking (and talking) round Shibden to try to locate the site of Anne's moss hut.

2019 Acknowledgements. Thanks again to Chris Ratcliffe for keeping this book in print for sixteen years and now for producing not only an eBook but also this new paperback edition.

Main Characters

Lister Household: Shibden Hall
Anne Lister, born 1791, inherited the estate from her Uncle James, 1826
Marian Lister, born 1798, Anne's sister
Aunt Anne Lister, born 1765, Anne's aunt
Jeremy Lister, born 1752, Anne's father
Elizabeth Cordingley, maidservant
George (Joseph Booth), manservant
John Booth, manservant and gardener
Rachel, Hemingway & others

Aristocratic Stuart Circle
Lady Stuart, London
Lady Stuart de Rothesay, wife of the recent ambassador to Paris
Vere Hobart, great-niece of Lady Stuart; married Captain Donald
Cameron in July 1832, and became Lady Cameron
Lady Gordon, friend of Lady Stuart
Hon James Stuart Wortley, Lady Stuart's nephew; Tory candidate for
Halifax, Dec 1832

York Circle Of Female Friends
Mariana Belcombe, born 1790, married Charles Lawton in 1816, lived
at Lawton, Cheshire
Belcombe family, York (Minster Court), including Mrs Belcombe and
her daughter Louisa
Dr Henry (Steph) Belcombe
Isabella Norcliffe, born 1785, lived with the Norcliffe family at Langton
Hall

The Walkers Of Lightcliffe
Ann Walker, born 1803, lived at Lidgate on the edge of the family's
Crow-nest estate
Aunt Anne Walker, born 1757, lived at Cliff-hill on the Crow-nest
estate
Elizabeth Walker, born 1801, Ann Walker's sister, married to Captain
Sutherland, lived in Scotland

Other Members of the Walker Family
William Priestley, born 1779, Ann Walker's older cousin and co-trustee,
lived at New House, Lightcliffe
Eliza (Mrs) Priestley, married William Priestley in 1808; friend of Anne

Lister
Henry Edwards, Ann Walker's uncle and co-trustee, lived at Pye-nest, Sowerby Bridge
Henry Edwards junior, Ann Walker's cousin, Pye-nest
Stansfield Rawson, cousin by marriage to Ann Walker, lived in Huddersfield
Jeremiah Rawson, manufacturer, Stansfield's brother, lived in Halifax
Christopher Rawson
Mr and Mrs Atkinson, Ann Walker's aunt and uncle
Waterhouse family, distant relatives, lived at Well-head, Halifax

Friends of Ann Walker

Catherine Rawson, daughter of Stansfield Rawson
Harriet Parkhill, a nosey gossip
Lydia Wilkinson, daughter of a local head-master, Halifax
Mr Fraser, suitor, died July 1832
Reverend Thomas Ainsworth and his wife

Professional Men

Reverend Musgrave, Vicar of Halifax
Dr Kenny, Mr Sutherland and Mr Day, local doctors
James Briggs, steward for Shibden estate, died Sept 1832
Samuel Washington, became land steward for Shibden estate
Joseph Stocks, neighbouring landowner at the head of Shibden valley
William Throp, nurseryman, Halifax

Key Shibden Workers and Tenants

John Bottomley, tenant of 9 acres, had vote in the new Halifax borough
Charles Howarth (and his son James), tenant, Ireland
Jonathan Mallinson, Stag's Head inn, Mytholm
Thomas Pearson, Denmark
George and Mary Robinson, Lower Brea, and wire mill
Joseph Pickles (and his sons George, John and Robert), worked on landscaping Shibden
James Holt, coal agent

Anne Lister's Abbreviations

M	- Mariana Lawton
Miss H	- Vere Hobart
Lady G	- Lady Gordon
Lady S	- Lady Stuart
Lady S- de R	- Lady Stuart de Rothesay
I. N	- Isabella Norcliffe
W. P	- William Priestley
Mrs W. P	- Mrs William Priestley
Miss W	- Ann Walker
J. R	- Jeremiah Rawson
Charles H	- Charles Howarth
H-x	- Halifax

INTRODUCTION
Anne Lister in 1832

It is May 1832. Anne Lister was making her way home, betrayed once again – by another woman's marriage plans. During winter 1831-32 she had set up house in Hastings with Vere Hobart. Anne Lister had looked to this well-connected young woman to fulfil her long-held romantic ambitions. But suddenly, Vere had rebuffed all Anne's hopes by accepting the proposal of her suitor, Captain Donald Cameron. The two women quickly parted, Anne heading for the north and for home.

Feeling bitterly betrayed, Anne Lister knew that her romantic youth was over. She was forty-one. So many of her female friends had married and settled for conventional lives as wives and mothers. A lesbian, she steadfastly rejected this for herself. And, as she departed the south, Anne revisited other 'old flames'[1] - Lady Gordon with whom she had flirted; and especially Mariana Belcombe (who in 1816 had married an older wealthy landowner, Charles Lawton; as Mariana Lawton she had, in Anne's eyes, 'sold her person to another for a carriage and a jointure…. for the sake of fixing her importance by being the mother of an heir to Lawton'[2]). Yet, over the intervening years, the two women had continued their doomed love affair. But now, jilted again, Anne Lister despaired of ever finding the life-companion she had so long sought. Her dazzling high-society ambitions - in Paris, London and now in Hastings - had crashed to earth.

On Monday 7 May, Anne reached home: Shibden Hall, built in the early fifteenth century near Halifax in the West Riding of Yorkshire. Anne had inherited the estate on the death of her uncle, James Lister, in 1826. However, under the terms of Uncle James'

---

[1] AL, 28.9.1832

[2] *I Know*, p 57.

will, his own brother and sister – Anne's aunt and elderly father – not only were entitled to share the Shibden rents with Anne (one-third each), but were also given the right to live at the Hall.[3] So not only her old-soldier father but also her own irksome younger sister Marian, became entitled to live in her home. Shortly after Uncle James' death, Anne, feeling restless, had set off for France.

Over the next few years, Anne (joined for some of the time by her aunt) lived in Paris. Anne had earlier received an excellent science education; and in Paris she studied geology and natural history, attending lectures by leading French anatomist Georges Cuvier - who in pre-Darwinian science, was at the cutting-edge in his study of fossils and extinct species.[4] Meanwhile, through Sibella MacLean, a well-connected friend, Anne had escorted to Paris Sibella's young niece, Vere Hobart; and so she met Vere's great-aunt, elderly Lady Stuart – and through Lady Stuart, *her* daughter-in-law (Lady Stuart de Rothesay, wife of the ambassador in Paris), as well as Lady Gordon - who had talked airily of their wintering together in Rome. Back in Britain, Anne could enjoy this newly-acquired élite circle of female friendship. Icarus-like, she had entertained plans to enter high society. But, with Vere's engagement in April 1832, these heady ambitions came crashing down.

*

Now back at Shibden, Anne Lister found that, with Marian behaving irritatingly like 'cock of the dung-hill',[5] it scarcely felt like home. The Listers might be landed gentry; but, after Paris, London and even Hastings, the Shibden household seemed distinctly provincial, threadbare and – worse still – spoke with a Yorkshire accent. Entitled to only one-third of the rents, Anne could not even afford a carriage. Feeling forlorn and melancholy, she spent long

---

[3] For discussion of the inheritance, see *FF*, especially pp 20-2.

[4] Eg Cuvier and his *Discours sur la Théorie de la Terre* (1825) argued that the Biblical Flood was merely the most recent of many catastrophes.

[5] AL, 23.3.1832.

lonely hours in Shibden's small but well-stocked library, reading the latest literature on geology, mineralogy and - increasingly - horticulture. And she continued to cast around among her extensive network of female friends for a life-partner with whom to settle.

All the while she was obliged by conventional social expectations to feign to Lady Stuart, Lady Stuart de Rothesay and others her delight at Vere's wedded happiness, her warm approval of Captain Cameron, and to follow their marriage plans - so bitterly reminiscent of Mariana's marriage to Charles Lawton nearly twenty years earlier. She held low spirits at bay only by drawing upon her own extensive resources: her indomitable will and energy; her scholarship and width of reading; her very practical hands-on estate management skills; her talent for visiting congenial female friends across North Yorkshire; her unshakeable belief in herself, and in 'my oddity' that 'nature taught me'; and her daily journal-writing, confiding to her diary in vivid detail all that she was doing, thinking, feeling. And so she managed to survive. Until on 6 July, when a chance re-acquaintance with neighbouring heiress Ann Walker changed all that.

*

The main narrative here, starting on 15 April, is followed in detail from mid-summer to 31 December. It tracks the story recorded in Anne Lister's diary of her emotional and erotic journey from betrayal at Hastings, back via London and home, to Ann Walker's unexpected July visit. Much of this account Anne wrote in her own secret code (here distinguished by *italics*), partly because it was so very intimate, and partly because so many of the Walker relations – William Priestley, his wife and the Rawsons - knew Anne Lister of old as not only an enthralling but also as a predatory woman; so, although there was then no polite language in which to talk about lesbianism, they were watchful.[6] For Ann Walker was not only young and shy; she had also inherited a small fortune from her

---

[6] FF, p18 & AL, 8,10, 1832. *FF*, pp ix-xviii, 249-51.

father, one of the prosperous mercantile-manufacturing families in the Halifax area.[7]

Once Anne Lister had returned home – to a Shibden she now found old-fashioned, inconvenient and draughty - two other narrative threads become also interwoven. First, inspired in part by her travels, her reading and by visiting her friends' elegant houses, she decided that Shibden must be remodelled. But, with a shorter purse than her grand friends, she turned her attention first to a less costly option: redesigning the part of the estate most visible from the house - a patchwork of pocket-handkerchief fields sloping immediately down for about a quarter of a mile to a small brook. From the Pennine uplands, Red Beck picturesquely flowed – and sometimes over-flowed - down the Shibden Valley and into the River Calder. Anne Lister spent solitary hours in the library, her wide scientific reading now encompassing not only current horticultural journals but also up-to-the-minute landscape-gardening literature, so popular among the landed gentry. In the era following 'Capability' Brown and the banishment of formality in gardens, Anne absorbed the new landscape popularisers - notably John Claudius Loudon.[8] She was soon filling her diary pages with dense agricultural details, as she commanded a small army of men to heave and dig, plant and cart soil for her, and as she began to shape nature to her desire – by disciplining one of Red Beck's boggier curves, and by rooting up the ancient agricultural hedges spoiling the leisured view from Shibden.

The second briefer story tracks Anne Lister's electoral activity from summer 1832, with the political tumult over the passing of the great Reform Bill. When it finally was enacted, Halifax became one

---

[7] *FF*, pp 28-35.

[8] John Claudius Loudon (1783-1846) is better known for his later writings for a domestic middle-class readership (eg *The Suburban Gardener* and *Villa Companion*, 1838); but his earlier books had a larger canvas (eg *Observations on the Formation and Management of Useful & Ornamental Plantations...& on Gaining the Embanking Land from Rivers...*, 1804).

of the new parliamentary boroughs entitled to elect two MPs, and more men gained the right to vote. Anne Lister's coercion of her enfranchised male tenants is fairly well known.[9] But it is worth reminding ourselves that a land-owning woman like Anne Lister (although kept unenfranchised by inclusion of the word 'male' in the Act) really could exert considerable electoral pressure. Not only was she landlord to her tenants, but she was also employer, plus an influential local patron (and was even beginning to develop as an industrial entrepreneur, for Shibden to provide coal for the rapidly urbanising town of Halifax).

*

In these few crucial months, with her personal ambitious plans defeated, Anne Lister returned home – and proceeded to turn herself from one person into another: from a traveller and high-society flirt into the commanding owner of ancient Shibden Hall. As she surveyed her Pennine domain, she determined to reshape the local landscape - and to embark upon a serious and prudent courtship that could change her life. In all, her indomitable will encouraged her to mould nature to her powerful desires.

---

[9] eg *FF*, pp. 45-9.

1. PROLOGUE
Betrayal: 15 April – 7 May

Anne Lister had set up house with Vere Hobart in Hastings. Although the younger woman often seemed coolly unresponsive, Anne and Vere happily enjoyed music and backgammon, visits out in the pony-carriage along the south coast, meeting other well-connected women.[10] There was even discussion, despite the threat of cholera, of their travelling abroad together.

Anne, intellectually restless, continued her wide reading of both current literature and reviews of the latest geology.[11] With her troublesome sister Marian running the household at Shibden, Anne certainly entertained no plans of returning home. Hastings raised her hopes for the future. Then came a long and tragic day which left her devastated.

> **Sunday 15** Mr West preached 33 minutes from 1 Timothy 1, 15 – queer evangelical sermon – *awake all the time* – went out at 11/2 for 11/2 hour – *met Captain Cameron – she asked him to dinner – the murder is out – we talked it over – she will not say 'no' – so it is done….*
>
> *Twenty minutes with Miss H-, laughing and joking, but found the tears starting as I kissed her forehead and ran away. 'What, are you going?' said she – but I was off, saying, 'Oh, I dare not look behind me'. A few tears are falling, but away with them –'For human weal [happiness], heaven husbands all events'. I am satisfied I can keep up the friendship – try to arrange* [a relationship] *with Lady Gordon & be better off than with Miss H-.*
>
> 'Tis striking 6 – dressed – dinner at 63/4. *On going down, saw them on*

---

[10] eg AL, 13.4.1832; 24 & 29.3.1832 on Lady Anne Scott (& botany).

[11] eg AL, 29.3.1832 for Mrs Trollope; 31.3.1832 for a review of Charles Lyell's *Principles of Geology*, volume 2, published Jan 1832, which considered the origin of each species, & why some became extinct. It was also the time (27.12.1831) that 23-year-old Charles Darwin set out on his 5-year voyage on the *Beagle*; Darwin took Lyell's first volume with him, and the second did not reach him until Nov 1832.

the sofa together & both looking so satisfied, I suspected how it was.[12] *The moment we left the dining-room about eight, he staying behind quarter-hour, she told me it* [uncertainty about his proposing?] *was all over - he made his offer in a very flattering manner to her, done it very well & she had accepted him. I said...I was very glad of it. She gave me her two cheeks to kiss. I kissed both, first one then the other, but said nothing – she moralized a little – said how a moment changed our whole lives, but she thought she should not repent. He stays tomorrow – I asked if he would dine with us – 'yes'...*[13]

He came in – we soon had coffee – I poured it out, ordered tea in half an hour & soon came upstairs – a little before nine - & left them to their happiness. What a sudden change for us all – for me too. She will go to Italy, but not with me. Well, tho' I made my eyes very red with crying before dinner, I already begin to think it is better – she would have left me in the lurch... Well, my prospects are changed.

It was a world, so well depicted by Jane Austen, of women *waiting* for a proposal of marriage that would change their lives. Until the offer was made, it could not be relied upon. Vere's engagement completely changed not only her prospects but those of Anne Lister too. She felt deeply wounded: in the diary even her handwriting, usually very firm, seemed to falter. The constipation she suffered scarcely helped, and Anne became gloomily anal.

But, as so often at such times, Anne Lister could fall back for solace upon both her daily journal-writing and her carefully-crafted correspondence with élite women like Lady Stuart, and with intimate friends like Mariana Lawton and Lady Gordon.

Monday 16 *Cried & sobbed bitterly for an hour last night, then began to be more composed, but could not sleep till three – awoke about six - up at seven – to the pot – long very thick piece with some difficulty...*

[More] *composed this morning... I neither want her pity nor her ridicule, both* [of] *which I might count upon, did she* [but?] *know my folly. Well, one word has made greater separation between us than thousands of miles could have done. She is no longer anything to me. My eyes are swelled up – I am*

---

[12] 'Sofa', deriving originally from Arabic, still suggested oriental luxury.

[13] In her despair, the accuracy of AL's coded sections sometimes falters.

not fit to be seen. Perhaps washing will do good. But I shall get over it....
How much I have written! But it has amused & done me good.

Wednesday 18 *She said we now clashed more than ever. However, it came out when I said Donald was a lucky man, that she thought I said... I thought she was making a <u>mésalliance</u>, & I might give that impression to others... 'Oh ho', thought I, 'she wants me to write in his praise to Lady S-.' The fact is, she knows she shall not like his mother & sisters - she wishes not for much of their company among her own friends - she is more in love with the novelty & niceness of being married than with Donald himself & she is shockingly touchy...*

I shall go well enough now. She has a dammed bad temper – suspicious, jealous, incredulous - I am far better without her.

Margin: *...God grant me to be happier with someone else.*

On Easter Monday, 23 April, just eight days after the betrothal, the two women left Hastings for London and Lady Stuart's. The following day they finally parted.

Where should Anne Lister head for? She had ambitious travel plans, but the emotional upheaval and bitter disappointment now soured everything. Every other diverting activity she could normally rely upon had paled. She was even losing her appetite. Anne made some rapid last-minute plans about where to go. She would casually call upon Lady Gordon near Cheltenham, upon Mariana at Lawton in Cheshire – and then perhaps home.

Sunday 29 *In 25 minutes, wrote 3 pages to my aunt to say... 'Now, all things considered, thought it best to attend to business concerns [at Shibden] without further loss of time – should be at Lawton tomorrow night – would write from there as soon as I could say when to expect me at Shibden.... Beg my father & Marian not to mention expecting me – wish to arrive unlooked for by all but yourself.'*

But the visit to Lady Gordon did not go quite according to plan. At lunch, Anne found her appetite had disappeared.

Lady G- talked of our travelling together, being in the same house but different apartments etc - in fact, different establishments & independent of each other.... I felt myself in reality gauche &, besides, in a false position. I have difficulty enough as to the usages of high society – and feeling unknown. But I have ten times more [gaucheries] *on account of money. Had I the five thousand a year Miss H- thought of* [ie thought I had]*, I could do. As it is, how can I? Yet there is none, not even M-, to whom I can really tell the whole thing as it is. My high society plans fail - unknown & without connections, money should abound. I have had my <u>whim</u> - tried the thing - & pretty much it has cost me. I shall in future perhaps do more wisely & within my compass. My pride needs not be much wounded – for none needs guess the truth. M- will attribute all* [ie everything] *to my affection for her. Miss H- will put it* [down]*, in some sort, to my care & disappointment about her. All the rest will never dream it is want of fortune, & I shall now get out of my scrape as well as I can, & can manage it tolerably.*

I have been an Icarus – but shall fall less fatally, for I can still live & be happy, providence being willing. I shall hear what M- says, & perhaps may go [to Italy?] *with Lady G-, & make up my mind* [not] *to spend more than I ought for the present, & then back quietly out. Well, I have gained experience - Lord, have mercy on me. I will eventually hide my head somewhere or other - I have fortune enough for that - & I shall be happier than now. I am glad to have seen Lady G, it has done me good - the mortification of feeling my gaucheries* [was] *wholesome – I shall now settle upon something & be better....*

Anne set off from Cheltenham northwards, observing the picturesque countryside, but wishing she was in better spirits to appreciate it.

Musing on my failure – resolved to give up all fine-society schemes, & planning what to do. May never see Miss H- or Lady G- or any of them again. Will talk to M-... Settle on fixing at Clermont or Grenoble... have a house & a garden & a study & be out of the way of English people....[14]

Get someone who will act [as] *maid & companion - have horses & light carriage & travel...*[15]

Lady G-'s proposal to be independent of each other opened my eyes – she would not be pothered by having me to '<u>society for</u>' in Florence... I may bury

[14] For an aristocratic parallel, see Amanda Foreman, *Georgiana: Duchess of Devonshire* (1998), pp 276-80, studying mineralogy in Lausanne, & climbing Vesuvius.

[15] Here, AL introduced her *dame de compagnie* scheme as an option if she travelled alone, without her aunt or M-.

> *myself somewhere in comfortable seclusion, & study - & then I shall have fortune enough for happiness. This determining did me good. What a change in all my plans & thoughts since this day fortnight - Donald's offer & [its] being accepted changed all. But I am already convinced it is for the best.*

> *At the Lion, Kidderminster at 8 50/" – boiled milk instead of tea – could not take it – got down 1/2 a muffin... What a comfort [are] my journals, how I can write in crypt all as it really is, & throw it off my mind & console myself - thank God for it.*

Anne Lister's visit to Lawton did not go well either. Mariana's reception was cool: she was preoccupied with her local philanthropy and family affairs. (Indeed, rather like comfortably old friends, the two women now spent much time discussing their wills.) Mariana talked about how she could not leave Charles, who might live for twenty years. By comparison, Anne's whimsical travel plans and unsettled state were becoming increasingly visible. Even conventionally-married Mariana suggested that 'I should be more happy settled than wandering about as I do now'.[16]

It was during this unsatisfactory visit to Lawton, the final nail in the coffin of Anne's high hopes and social ambitions, that she developed her *dame de compagnie* scheme. This translated literally as 'lady companion', but it carried a rich set of social nuances: not quite a servant, not quite like a governess, yet not a social equal as the companionship had to be *paid* for. And, with Anne Lister's reputation among her female friends, it carried additional possible meanings. However, Mariana, perhaps feeling sympathetic to Anne's low spirits, responded helpfully to the scheme: she offered her own sister Louisa Belcombe for the post, and even agreed to write to her – but conspiratorially, as if the suggestion had *not* originated from Anne.

---

[16] AL, 29.4.1832.

May 1832

Tuesday 1 *M- came to bed to me for forty minutes – but no thought or word of love on either side… [I] proposed taking my aunt & living in France at Clermont or Grenoble – or asking Charlotte Norcliffe – or taking* [Mariana's acquaintance] *Miss Salmon as <u>dame de compagnie</u> & to act as my maid. M- proposed her sister Louisa for this instead of Miss Salmon - talked it over. M- to write & ask Lou – but as if from M- herself, unknown to me.*

Wednesday 2 *Wrote 3 pages & ends to Miss H-, very affectionate but proper letter that she might read aloud - left her to guess whom & what I thought of most…*

Came upstairs at 11 50/" - had M- a little while - talking quietly… Was she glad to see me? 'Yes', said she, 'I am - & if we were living together, we should be happy – and if Charles was a reasonable person, we should be as well with him as without him – for a man is always of some use'. I merely & quietly answered, 'I should not be so happy with him'.

Well, I certainly never saw anyone so changed as M- since I was here last - as for anything like love, she does not seem to feel a grain of it. We have sunk down to all but common friendship - & from this moment I shall, without remorse, suit my convenience – do better, if I can… M-might have revived my affection in this visit - she has probably set its last remains at rest for ever - & here I am, at forty-one, with a heart to seek. What will be the end of it? Heaven protect & guide me!

F53° in my bedroom now at 12 20/". I wore her ring on my left third finger on arriving & yesterday morning, but in the evening changed it to my right finger – today have laid it aside altogether - she has not made any remark on the subject.

Anne's hopes of her relationship with Mariana faded. And as they faded, the narrative began to entwine with two other threads: Anne's continued involvement in Vere Hobart's imminent marriage to Donald Cameron (and the convention of a legal marriage settlement between the two families), so reminiscent of Mariana's much earlier marriage; and Anne's planning her *dame de compagnie* scheme, with her eye especially on Mariana's sister, Louisa Belcombe. Mariana did write to Louisa about her travelling with Anne. But their mother, Mrs Belcombe, was of course protective of her daughters' respectability, and she knew Anne Lister of old.

However, Anne resourcefully dredged up from the recesses of her memory allusion to a ducal connection to enhance the social plausibility of her scheme.

> **Sunday 6** *Sat with M- (who was lying on her sofa) till 11 25/" – she had had a letter from her sister Louisa; & I letter from Miss H-…. Donald had had a letter from his father approving his marriage & sending his respects to the young lady, but saying not a word on business [ie the marriage settlement] or doing anything for him.*
>
> *Louisa had shewn M-'s letter to Mrs Belcombe – who…[protested] at her being a humble companion. But she [Louisa] herself seemed differently inclined & asked what I requested. M- & I talked this over tonight - I said Lady S- de R- had offered me the grand-daughter of a duke of Ancaster (forgot her name – see my journal of two years ago) as <u>dame de compagnie</u>.*

Anne left Mariana with a few regrets. Yet it was difficult finally to shake off this old relationship: the two women just could not ever say a final goodbye.

> **Monday 7** *Off from Lawton at 11 55/"… Musing – read a little French vocabulary – slept a very little. At Manchester at 4 – 1/4 hour delayed at Rochdale for horses - got out there – changed shoes & gaiters to be ready for walking, but 4 horses to the [top] of Blackstone Edge (the 6 miles) trotted the whole way up the hill, & at the top in 40 minutes! Came forwards with a pair of horses [downhill to Sowerby Bridge] – walked from the Causey to King Cross turnpike, & afterwards up the New Bank to Shibden, & arrived at 8 25/". Found all well & as usual – dinner at 9 – my aunt came & sat with me – just wished my father & Marian good night – came to my room at 10 – siding [ie putting away] & tidying 1/2 hour – fine day – F63° in my bedroom (blue room) now at 10 1/2 pm.*

Shibden was now Anne's only remaining retreat. And, returning defeated, she had wanted as quiet a home-coming as possible.

Anne Lister's diary page: 12-15 May 1832

2. HOMECOMING
8 May - 17 June

Anne had ensured that her return was unremarked: in the event it was more low-key than even she had intended. The very coolness of her reception must have thrown her. For Marian Lister, Anne's homecoming was the return of the prodigal elder daughter. Marian, looking after their elderly father, held sway over Shibden's domestic regime. Between the two sisters little love was lost. The arguments – as so often, when so much was at stake – pivoted around the seemingly insignificant (here, arrangements about the Lister pew in Halifax Parish Church).

For Anne, everything had changed since her journey northwards. The Pennine landscape of home even required a different, more practical dress code. The estate needed her attention; for James Briggs, the steward responsible for managing affairs during her long absences, was now seriously ill – and *someone* needed to take charge.

Yet Anne felt even more rootless.[17] But at least, she now could draw upon the resources of the local landscape and upon Shibden's excellent library to provide intellectual stimulation. She also sought solace in her correspondence with her well-connected women friends (spending no less than five hours letter-writing one day), though her letters, of course, seldom reflected how isolated and melancholy she really felt.

MAY 1832

Tuesday 8 Very fine morning, F61o at 11 am in my room – long while in dressing – in getting out my Shibden habiliments [ordinary clothes] (pelisse etc) to put on. Breakfast at 11 – my aunt with me – sat talking above an hour – *she obscurely hinted at my getting some place in England: 'There is all England for you to be in'. Said I had calculated all ways – it would not do – must go abroad – would rather go to America than stay in*

---

[17] Even her handwriting looked frail.

England. This seemed to stagger her – I took no more notice. Said M- was changed to[wards] me – I was no longer the first object of her thought - & it was therefore unlikely we should come together – thought hers not a good life, nor did she seem to desire it to be.

Came to my room soon after 12 – wrote (3 pages & ends & under the seal) to Miss H-, & a half-sheet (& 1 page & ends of envelope) to Lady Stuart, till 4 – then till 5 10/" wrote the whole [journal] of yesterday & so far of today. Nice enough easy & affectionate letter to Miss H-… 'I shall burn your letters as you desire & I promised, & you will burn mine – we are both of us quite at ease on this point' – say I am better than I have felt for weeks – 'the breezes of my own native hills certainly do me good' … 'Lady S- will tell you of my dame de compagnie scheme etc – I must be sometime here – *you know how gladly I would flee away & be at rest or in motion elsewhere.'*

Nice easy chit-chat letter to Lady S-, …necessary to come home on the score of business – my steward in bad health – could not easily replace… Mention… my idea of 'a clever, sensible dame de compagnie, who would do all the little [services] I care for in the Lady's-maid way, & go abroad with me to all the outlandish places I wish to see…[18] What do you … think of this plan? …

Dinner at 6 20/" – my aunt came & sat with me… Went out at 8 for 3/4 hour – along the walk to the mill at Mytholm & back[19] – very well satisfied. Sat talking in the little sitting room – Marian & I got to almost quiet sparring about her leaving the seat [ie family pew] unlocked at church - as we always do whenever the subject is mentioned. *Well, I wish I could avoid saying anything – we shall never agree – the less we see of each other the better – I like her less & less. I must get away somewhere – the money is the thing – I must invent something or other very shortly - but off I must go.* Came to my room at 10 10/" – fine day tho' threatening rain all day & a few drops as I came in this evening – F59o in my room at 111/2 pm.

---

[18] Here, AL explains the scheme in terms of her servant, Cameron, leaving. Her travel plans were constrained by the recent outbreak of cholera.

[19] George Robinson's water-powered wire mill at one point employed 200 children, *FF* p 51.

Marian was increasingly resentful of her daunting elder sister. Anne referred disdainfully to her immediate family merely as 'them all' in her diary. Her *dame de compagnie* scheme symbolised both her desire to find a more companionable relationship, and her desire still to flee to 'outlandish places'.

Meanwhile, her first visit across Shibden had taken her along 'the walk' which ran down the broad sweep of fields below the house to Red Beck and a small bridge.[20] On this occasion it took her down to Mytholm. Here rural industry, conveniently tucked out of view from Shibden, alerted Anne to the industrial potential of small-scale coal-mining on her land.

The walk, which acquired increasing symbolic power for Anne, was the most direct way by foot out eastwards to Lightcliffe and to her old friends, William Priestley and his wife.

> **Wednesday 9** Reading my newspaper (Courier) & dressing till 10 10/"... lay awake musing this morning as yesterday – but still in better spirits than of late – perhaps my nerves [ie courage] will get braced up again...by & by. About an hour at breakfast talking to my aunt – out at about 11 1/4 in the walk. Mr Sunderland came about 12 & took out the tooth (right, 1st double tooth) I had so much trouble with in Paris...
>
> Went out again (having plugged the gum with cotton wool steeped in eau de cologne) at 1 - down the walk, & by the Lower Brea road to Lightcliffe. Long talk with Jack Green by the way - might put down a small water-wheel where Jonathan Mallinson has made his pigsties,[21] for about £200, & the water would run from the Mytholm mill - might employ 4 colliers, & supposing them to get 20 loads a day apiece, at 6d per load, & allow 1/2 for expense & say that I might clear £300 a year.

[20] It is unclear the exact line of 'the walk'. The 1791 map (similarly, the 1854 OS map) marks a thick line of trees running from the far end of the Shibden garden down alongside the fields (Hall Ing, Calf Croft, Lower Brook Ing) to the large bend in Red Beck. At this point, there was very probably a small bridge across to Tilly-holm, Daisy Bank & Lower Brear; however, the later enormous railway embankment makes tracing the precise 'walk' tricky.

[21] By the Stag's Head inn, Mytholm.

> Mrs Priestley not at home – at her school – sat with her there from 2₁/₂ to 3₁/₂, chit-chat – then walked home with her for a minute or 2 – just saw Mr P-, & off home at 3₃/₄ - sauntered about the fields...

> Sat talking to my aunt about Shibden – its forlorness etc etc till 8 – from then to 9 40/" with them all in the little room & then came upstairs – wrote all the above of today – feel better for air & exercise & ate my dinner with more appetite than I have done for some time.

So the structure of Anne Lister's days back at Shibden took shape. She ate her meals quickly, on her own or with her aunt – rather than with 'them all'. (The arguments with Marian now moved from pew-keys to more contentious will-writing, and who would leave the other sister anything.) She reacquainted herself with Shibden's fields and farms and tenants; and she caught up again with old friends like Mrs Priestley.

But her restlessness remained. She must travel. She planned a visit through the North Riding to the Dalton family, relations of the Norcliffes, at Croft Rectory near Darlington. Arranging this Yorkshire trip prompted more letter-writing. On her way back, Anne would stay with the Norcliffes - and possibly at York, but she seemed indecisive about the precise dates of the York visit. Then, in a melancholy letter to Mariana, which was unusually honest, it became clear that Anne still pinned her hopes on Louisa Belcombe becoming her companion.

> **Thursday 10** Long talk with Marian – she will not leave me anything – I shall go & make my will & not name her. Went to my room at 4 ... wrote 3 pages to M-... My mind is for ever wandering to other subjects – the Reform bill, & its early-omened fate.... All that would have interested me so deeply, is brushed off from my mind as easily as dust from polished steel – I am sick of the whole world – and the sight of my will made [ie completed] will give me more pleasure than anything else.

> Ask to hear from her... if she has any chance of hearing from her sister [Louisa]. 'Sometimes I fancy this scheme interests me – then I care not for it one straw... I think I cannot remain here long... but the air of my own native hills has done me good; &, spite of fate, the shades of Shibden have still some charm for me... Ever, my dearest

Mary, very especially & entirely yours, A. L-.'

From Paris, Anne had followed the progress of the Reform Bill with keen interest.[22] The Bill was still opposed by the conservative House of Lords: on Tuesday, the Whig Prime Minister, Lord Grey, had asked William IV to create new peers; on Wednesday, the King objected; Grey and his ministers then resigned. Anne avidly read the newspapers, and spent solitary hours writing letters to her Tory friends, Lady Stuart, Lady Stuart de Rothesay - and, in rather stilted prose, to Vere Hobart. For Anne, it was a painful, but necessary, hypocrisy to have to write such conventional betrothal sentiments to Vere.

> **Friday 11** Breakfast at 10 20/" & read the Courier – ministers out – joy go with them – we have had enough of my Lords Grey & Brougham...
>
> Chit-chat [letter] to the Lady Stuart – could not resist writing them a little word of congratulations on the change of ministry – the exit of my Lords Grey & Brougham & co... Wonder what Lady S- thinks of my <u>dame de compagnie</u> scheme – no hint about it to Lady S- de R-. Affectionate chit-chat [letter] to Miss H-: 'the praises you hear of him [Donald Cameron] delight me – but the greatest praise I have yet heard, & that which pleases me best, because it is joint, & equally deserved by you both, is from Lady Stuart: "they are [the] most amiable & agreeable lovers I ever saw" – this quite delights me'.

In her long letter to Mariana, subterfuge was piled upon subterfuge:

Anne could *not* be seen to have taken the initiative.

> **Saturday 12** Read the Courier – nothing known of the new ministry... Then wrote 3 pages to M- ... On the subject of her sister: 'the sooner this matter is settled one way or other the better; for as I cannot well remain very long here, I must fix upon something very shortly. If Louisa seems to have any inclination for the thing [ie the dame scheme], do you not think she had better, on seeing me, ask me to walk – and take that opportunity of gently broaching the subject herself. She can inquire [of] my plans, cautiously make me an offer as

---

[22] AL, eg 27.2.1832, see *FF*, p 45.

if nothing had ever passed [between me and you] about it... I shall probably be in York on Monday fortnight – what do you think [of] this? ...I have had a very kind letter from Lady S-; she wonders why I do not fix at once to join Lady G-. I think I am in too restless a humour – Shibden is certainly not improved in comfort to <u>me</u> – I long to wander a little, far from society & all its vanities – my mind is out of tune [with the times] – but I am better than I was, & trust to my natural elasticity of spirit for the rest – God bless you, Mary! I am, at all rates, very especially & entirely yours, A. L-.'

With her *dame de compagnie* scheme still uncertain, Anne had to fall back upon panglossian optimism, based on her religious faith, which she shared with Mariana.

Monday 14 Looking over maps – planning German tour – *counting upon having Louisa Belcombe - when letter came from her to M-, forwarded here with a few lines from M-....* Letter from M-, Lawton – she had been ill... She thinks my letter (that of Thursday) 'not a cheering one. Do not despond... surely you ought not to be "sick of all the world"... all things work together for good'. *Lou would have been glad of going with me - amazed at the manner in which her mother took it - hoped M- would talk her [mother] out of her scruples...* Perhaps, in this instance, all things have worked together for good, & now, as for ever, Providence serves me in spite of myself...

Read a little of the Courier – the Duke of Wellington to be prime minister & Mr Baring Chancellor of the Exchequer. Breakfast with my aunt at 10 1/4 - read the remainder of the Courier & staid talking till 12 – *a little about M- (said not a word of the plan about Louisa) – the less we talked on the subject the better. I was annoyed & hurt, but it was wearing off - we [Anne & M-] should never perhaps suit [each other] again... but her mind was changed to me & mine was changing fast to her.*

Tuesday 15 At 9 1/4 among my books till breakfast at 10 3/4 - back again at 12, busy dusting and arranging till 6 – dinner at 6 10/" in 25 minutes... Then took up & finished my letter to M-... Hardly know what to make of Louisa's letter – conditional altogether - she hopes... she can prevail against the scruples [of her mother]... Finished my letter to M-, added nothing of moment – merely that the more I thought of the plan respecting her sister the less I thought it likely to answer – if mamma was less inflexible than usual, it was a great chance that things could be made agreeable...

Went downstairs at 8 – sat 3/4 hour with my aunt in the drawing room, then in the little room with them all till 9 50/" when came to my room.

Despite trying to appear unconcerned about Louisa Belcombe, Anne was near her lowest ebb. Even this craftily-devised scheme seemed likely to flounder.

She found solace in Shibden's rich cultural treasures – notably its library, whose books ranged from French and classical texts (both in translation and in the original), through science (including anatomy, chemistry and astronomy), sermons and theology, to travel and the journalism of the day.[23] For instance, on Wednesday 16 Anne spent an hour over breakfast reading the newspaper, half an hour on the terrace reading French vocabulary - and nine solitary hours in the library.

Thursday 17 Not dressed till 8 50/", busy with the books in my closet[24].... In the library all the day... Dinner at 6$_{1/2}$ in 3/4 hour... Then sat with them all (till came to my room at 10) – *all vulgar – my aunt the best, but with all her goodness to me, sadly tiresome as a companion - the rest insufferable in point of vulgarity – Marian's emphasis in speaking terrible...*

Met Mrs Robinson of Lower Brea who said the town was like a fair – the people had a bonfire of almost (or quite) 3 cart-loads of coals for rejoicing at the so speedy return to office of Lord Grey & his colleagues – the Duke of Wellington not able to make a ministry [ie government].

Rejecting Wellington as premier, people had stopped work. London had been plastered with posters urging them to withdraw money from the banks: 'To stop the Duke, go for gold.' On Tuesday

[23] *Catalogue of the Valuable Library of Books, Maps etc...to be sold by auction*, 1846 (SH:3/ L/92); eg first day's sale: Lot 135, Transactions of the Geological Society of London, 4 parts [no date], & Lot 139, 17 volumes of *Leeds Intelligencer* 1793-1831.

[24] Closet: a large cupboard or small room; possibly a storage recess in AL's bedroom (Blue Room) or, more likely the tiny study over the porch. John Lister (1936) gives slightly different names for some rooms.

15, Wellington had told the King he could no longer form a government.

Against this tumultuous backdrop, with Grey recalled and the Reform bill rescued, Anne planned her visit through Yorkshire. This prompted thoughts of travelling on to Scotland, of finding a companion, and of Louisa and Mariana.

Friday 18 *Incurred a cross thinking of M-.* Fine morning F58° now at $10_1/4$ - looking at my road book – the thought struck me of going from Croft to Edinburgh *to see the MacKenzies, Lady Elizabeth Thackray & Miss Hall – to try first for Miss MacK-. Thought of Miss Freeman & Miss Walker of Lidgate as people here. Louisa Belcombe & Miss Price in York, besides Miss Salmon. Surely I shall get some companion by-and-by.*

Letter [from M-]... *Thinks she* [Lou] *cannot mention the thing* [scheme] *to me, but I might to her, before* [ie in front of] *Mrs Belcombe, in such sort* [ie manner] *as to have more influence than by argument... M- thinks '... The plan agreeable to Lou, & I am sure you would like her society...'. I feel undecided whether to like the plan or not.... More kind & comfortable [letter] than I expected – but too late? I cannot forget her* [ie M-'s dis]*owning* [me] *– she would rather go on as at present than have any change - my own mind is not with her...*

Breakfast at $10_1/2$ - off at $11_3/4$, over the hill to Stoney Royde [Halifax] – an hour in getting there, latterly over several walls – sat 40 minutes with Mrs Rawson[25]– rather an invalid – *tired of the history of her servants.* Then to Throp's – 3-foot oaks (that will be 4-foots) to be 50/- a thousand next November & 60/- the November following – sycamores the same, to be planted & upheld [ie supported], at 20/- per thousand.

Went to the bank – Mr [Christopher] Rawson not there - only £8 balance in my favour – desired nothing more to be paid on my account till after the rent day.

At the Saltmarshes about $1_1/2$ - stayed dinner... Long sit after dinner till tea time, talking despairing politics with Mr S-. Revolution certain by more or less sudden degrees – he has serious thoughts of investing money in the United States bank, or buying an estate in Canada & going there – land near York in Canada (not far from Montreal) at a

---

[25] Mother of Christopher, Stansfield and Jeremiah Rawson - and others.

dollar an acre some while ago, now at 3 dollars, so strong is the tide of emigration – all the Irish protestants going there....

The Times – read as I walked along – still demurs [ie hesitation] about the Grey ministry, the terms on which they return to, or retain, office.

Very kind letter too... from Miss Hobart, Richmond Park – no plan yet marked out – all in status quo [ie as before] - *high congratulatory praise of Donald from many quarters*... Miss H- does not approve my dame de compagnie scheme – this weighs with me.

Tories like Saltmarshe obviously felt the shadow of the guillotine hanging darkly over their bank deposits, and Anne increasingly shared these conservative political opinions. Her friends, like Vere Hobart, were scrupulous observers of social class and subtle gradations.

Saturday 19 From 12₃/₄ to 4, wrote 3 pages... to Miss H-; what a long letter! Politics – parading a straw figure of the king with a petticoat over his head (& then burning him) on Wednesday evening in Halifax.[26] Then came at 8 pm news they liked better and the church bells rang till 12 at night. Thursday, the town crammed & one of the largest bonfires ever seen, & [I added] 'the Duke of Wellington himself can do nothing for us now, unless, by drawing off his friends, he saves the house of peers [ie Lords] for some while longer'... Then all about the dame de compagnie scheme...

The Times newspaper again – the ministry still not finally settled – came to my room at 10 50/" having stayed talking to my aunt [and continued her letter to Vere]...

'You don't like it [the scheme] – you have no idea the impression that made on me... I will read Mrs Trollope[27] – but I don't mean to sit at table with the woman who does my dirty work – she [ie companion] is to do no work but help me to dress, to take care of my things, & make others do the rest – I shall only have her for travelling.... I want someone to speak to who is sensible, & comfortably well-mannered –

---

[26] AL, isolated up in Shibden and with newspapers arriving late, may only found this out two days afterwards.

[27] Probably Frances Trollope, *Domestic Manners of the Americans*, 1832, on Jacksonian frontier democracy.

that cannot be a lady's maid – I want someone who will go where I like. Is there a thoroughly independent person sufficiently like me to do that? Two <u>petticoat-bearers</u> are enough – a maid in addition would be one too many for her own happiness, & that of all the rest. What do you think? <u>You</u> can almost persuade me for or against anything.'

It was just at this point, perhaps buoyed up by writing to Vere Hobart, that Anne Lister began to find an important new sense of purpose, a renewed welling-up of energy. She began to develop ambitious improvement schemes for the Shibden estate, inspired by her travels and her reading of current gardening magazines. To put her grand plans into effect, she became a woman in a hurry. But first she had to persuade her increasingly deaf eighty-year-old father.

> **Sunday 20** Fine morning – F59$\frac{1}{2}$ at 9 – some time talking to my father about making window to open in the library passage, & about planting the top of the wheat-field (1st mentioned to him last night) with sycamores – nothing said against it – determined too (if [I am] here in November) to continue my walk along the brow in Tilly-holm to the foot-path.[28]
>
> Breakfast at 10$\frac{3}{4}$ in $\frac{3}{4}$ hour – then sauntering in the garden till 12 – then read aloud the whole morning service in 35 minutes & one of Mr Knight's sermons in 20 minutes - then asleep. Then read over (Marian's) No 8 of the <u>Horticultural Register</u> price 1/- monthly, by Joseph Paxton & Joseph Harrison[29] – good...
>
> In my letter to M-, said ... 'As to Louisa,... had there been no difficulty, I should have settled the thing at once, and been glad of it. As it is,...perhaps it will be best for you to reconcile mamma <u>provisionally</u>;... whether I can make a good opportunity [when in York] of saying any-thing bearing on the subject in a judicious way, is quite a chance.... I always mistrust my ground in the minster court [at the Belcombes']... Then walked 35 minutes on the terrace – <u>the Times</u> newspaper again – Lord Grey and his administration in, with an understanding of carrying the bill unmutilated.

---

[28] 'Holm' meant a low-lying meadow by a stream. Tilly-Holm was probably a narrow field running along Red Beck on the opposite bank from Lower Brook Ing.

[29] *Horticultural Register & General Magazine*, 1831-36 ie still very new.

> Letter… from Lady Stuart… All against my <u>dame de compagnie</u>
> scheme – thinks 1/2 maid & 1/2 companion will never do – says Lady
> Gordon seems disappointed that my plans are so unfixed. *Perhaps,*
> *after all, Lady G- & I will get together.*

The opposition to her *dame* scheme that Anne Lister now
encountered was, after all, hardly surprising. Her friends knew her
reputation only too well; and the scheme, with its notion of *paid*
companionship, was an undignified blurring of class lines for a
woman in their social circle.

So, with her tree-planting, Anne had half-unconsciously decided
to settle – and settle at Shibden. But first, the trip to North Yorkshire:
her farewell was as low-key as her home-coming.

> **Monday 21** Till 10 (undressed) packing – dressed – breakfast at 11
> with my aunt as usual in the drawing-room. Marian came to us for a
> few minutes – my father out – did not see him. Off from Shibden at 11
> 50/"… – along the Godley road – turned off at Wibsey (2 miles from
> Bradford) to Leeds, & changed horses… all among the flame & smoke
> of the Shelf, Wibsey, Low Moor, & Bradford (Bowling) iron foundries.
> Hilly from Leeds to Harrogate.

As she passed the entrance gates to Harewood House, Anne
admired its fine situation on the top of a 'considerable eminence' in
an extensive park. An experienced and observant traveller, she
stored up for later images of picturesque rocky gorges and
gothicised houses.

> **Tuesday 22** Off at 8₃/4 from Harrogate… No reading at all today –
> made the pencil notes of today, & amused myself with musing – *first*
> *of Lady Gordon – incline to her* – thinking, as I <u>often</u> do in travelling, of
> Shibden & alterations there – planting – making a road traversing
> along Bairstow… At 7₁/2 first peep at Croft bridge – how well it looks
> stretching across the broad Tees & the very valley itself! At the
> Rectory at 7 40/" – all out for the moment but Mrs James Dalton &
> Isabella Norcliffe - a nice enough welcome… Came to my room at 10
> 50/", I. N- came up with me & sat with me till 11 50/".

Isabella Norcliffe and Anne had long ago had been lovers. The
Norcliffes were county gentry, and Isabella, uncompromisingly
masculine, could be crudely out-spoken.

Wednesday 23 Dinner at 5₃/₄ - coffee – came to my room at 10 25/" &
I. N-staid with [me] till near 12… *Told her…all about M-…that I now no
longer expected our getting together… Vindicated myself against the
appellation Isabella says people give me – of tuft-hunter.*

Anne spent six days at Croft, and while there received a sobering
letter from Mariana:

Sunday 27 'With regard to Lou, perhaps you are right, had there been
no opposition, it [the scheme] might have done very well; but I don't
think it is worth taking any trouble about… It often occurs to me that
you had better trust to your southern friends for a companion – they
might or [might] not notice any of your own recommendations
[reputation], & perhaps they would be better pleased at your having a
friend of your own [rather] than one of them. You now have so little
to do with Yorkshire people that perhaps you had better not begin
again…' *Somehow this letter has given me but little pleasure.*

Worse still, Anne still suffered from constipation and had
developed a bad back.[30] Could her hopes and ambitions sink any
lower?

On Monday 28, she left Croft for York. Here at the Belcombes'
Minster Court, she sat with Louisa, another sister and Mrs Belcombe
– but for only fifteen minutes. She then left for the Norcliffes'
country house, Langton. From here, she wrote an account of the
York visit to Mariana Lawton:

Wednesday 30 1/4 hour in the minster court – [I made] no mention of
my travels [when] there, 'but… we somehow got into the subject… &
I soon found, from the manner in which the thing was handled, that
the wisest way was to yield, to own that a new light burst in upon me
– that they were probably right, my [dame] scheme was too
anomalous [ie irregular], & I should write to you today & give it up.
The fact is, I am convinced, both by your remarks & by the laughing
& quizzing here [at Langton], that…we had best think of it no more.
The sentence, "You have now so little to do with Yorkshire people,
that perhaps you had better not begin again", made me melancholy
the while – it forcibly brought to mind all I have often felt, &

---

[30] She also learnt of the death of George Playforth, manservant at Shibden; AL was
genuinely upset.

lamented over of late - I see all old connections so slipping from under me, that my eyes must be opened wide upon it now; & the sooner I set myself about being resigned & reconciled, the better. All this costs me a deeper sigh than even you imagine; but the truth flashes upon me at last – no effort of my own can save me; and all I can do is to submit – now & then, I am sadly out of sorts – but I am better certainly than I was; Croft & Isabella did me good; & I hope & flatter myself you will find no fault when you see me.'

JUNE 1832

So Anne had become something of a figure of fun among her friends in Yorkshire. In a letter to Vere Hobart, she assured Vere that she had 'quite done with' the *dame de compagnie* scheme: she did not think 'much real pleasure is to be had from bought society'.[31]

Generally, Anne lamented the passing of traditional ways, confiding to Isabella's younger sister Charlotte *'about the hum-bug of life – I had less independence than ever – the same people & things did not give the same pleasure as formerly'.*[32]

Certainly politics was changing. The Reform Bill, finally passed by the House of Lords, received royal assent on Thursday 7 June and became law. Among its less-publicised clauses was the insertion of the word 'male' into the new qualifications for the parliamentary franchise. Chiming with her mood of nostalgia for earlier days, Anne read Jameson's *Memoirs of Celebrated Female Sovereigns*.

> **Friday 8** Downstairs & breakfast at 10 40/" – letter from my aunt (Shibden) - Mrs N- had done breakfast but sat reading partly aloud the <u>Albion</u> newspaper... Sat long talking politics etc with Mrs N-, *saying women were not allowed to have any political rights – why should they care for politics?* Coffee – tea – read forward to Mary Queen of

---

[31] AL, 6.1832. Lady Stuart also wrote to congratulate her on giving up the *dame de compagnie* scheme.

[32] AL, 6.6.1832.

Scots & the middle of the reign of Elizabeth, volume 1, Mrs Jameson.[33]

Her aunt's letter told how her sister Marian had apparently opened a parcel addressed to 'Miss Lister' – to Anne's great annoyance.[34]

Tuesday 12 What nonsense! What folly in Marian to call herself 'Miss Lister' & thus make all this confusion!....

I should probably leave all society & go and live quietly – in Paris or somewhere – would not in any case spend more than a thousand a year – disappointed about M-, might not see much of her again.

Anne just could not forget Mariana, even though her worldly marriage was now almost twenty years earlier. However, while at Langton, she enjoyed flirting with Charlotte Norcliffe; then Isabella arrived from Croft.

Friday 15 1/2 hour alone with C. N-, talking of... *how much I wanted a fling – envied the liberty of going per diligence* [French coach].

Sat 16. *Tib slept with me... fine day... Rather sweet upon Charlotte tonight.*

Anne, with her talent for female intimacy, managed to enjoy tête-à-têtes with all the Norcliffe women.[35] But her emotional unsettledness remained. She could not remain a guest at Langton for ever. Would she spend the rest of her life at Shibden - and with whom?

---

[33] Anna Jameson, *Memoirs of Celebrated Female Sovereigns*, 1831; perhaps the recent constitutional snub linked to this 'golden age' nostalgia.

[34] The parcel contained steel dissecting instruments from Sheffield

[35] For an aristocratic parallel on the ease of fluid relationships and a free-wheeling bisexuality similar to AL's York circle, see Foreman, *Georgiana*, pp 166-7.

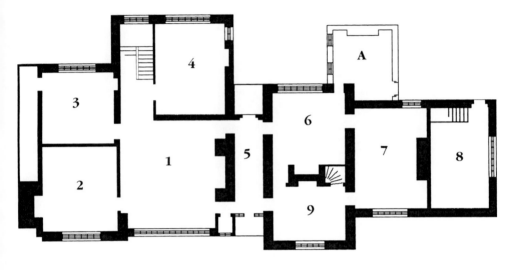

Ground floor plan, Shibden Hall,
as it might have been c 1832

1. Hall (housebody)
2. Drawing room?
3. North Parlour (little sitting-room or 'little room')
4. Buttery
5. Cross passage or library passage 6. Lower kitchen
7. Upper kitchen
8. Workshop
9. Study (now the library?)

3. THE LAND
Vere's Marriage Settlement: 18 June - 9 August

Anne Lister had given up her *dame de compagnie* scheme as 'too anomalous'. But while she was still at Langton, her correspondence with Vere Hobart offered her sharp insights into the real financial attractions to an impoverished man of marrying an heiress. She saw clearly how essential it was for a propertied bride to have a sound marriage settlement. It was this document, drawn up by lawyers, that settled property arrangements between the bride's and the groom's families. [36]

JUNE

Monday 18 Down to breakfast at 11 20/" – 4 pages... from Miss Hobart... *'My fortune is settled on myself, after deducting two thousand five hundred pounds paid down to him [Donald], & I am to have two hundred a year pin-money [paid by the husband to his wife for her personal use]. He hopes to be able to settle five hundred a year jointure [for her widowhood] – but my opinion's that the estate will not bear so much. However...my fortune may be considered as twenty-five thousand pounds – and you were but <u>little out</u> in your reckoning when you estimated it at a thousand a year – for if all [monies] were paid it would be to [ie within] a fraction nine hundred & eighty. But with the proposed sales for present purposes of outfit [cost of a carriage?] & other casualties [payments], I shall leave only a clear eight hundred a year, including my <u>brother</u> & <u>the pension</u> & the <u>pin-money</u>.[37] Of course, this is for your eye & <u>ear</u> alone & I hope will be burnt when you sufficiently understand it...'.*

Kind letter enough – the most so possible from her... Will she make Donald

---

[36] Without a marriage settlement, the bride was left at the mercy of an unscrupulous husband or his family; information had to be exchanged extremely discreetly between both sides; B. English & J. Saville, *Strict Settlement: a guide for historians*, Hull, 1983, p.36.

[37] A marriage settlement could also include provision for portions for other relatives; see J Perkin, *Women and Marriage in Nineteenth-Century England*, 1989, pp 65-70.

happy - & will she be so herself? She ought to be - she will not gain much else by it - his family needs not find fault with the settlements.[38]

Friday 22 *Making notes as yesterday from Norcliffe's tour [of northern capitals] - planning Isle of Wight tour for the Norcliffes – 3/4 hour tête-à-tête with C. N-; she advises me not to talk so much to mother of travelling, or so as to make her think me – as she does – an infidel & half-mad.*

Saturday 23 Kind letter... from Lady Gordon... *has no doubt of our suiting very well if our <u>stars</u> ever call us to the same part of the world & we <u>join forces</u>... 'I am very glad that you liked Miss Hobart's future [ie betrothed] – he looked to me narrow-chested & uncomfortable & <u>very</u> <u>Scottish</u>. Pray write to me'....* Out at 12 with Steel to fell the ash tree I had so begged to have down... Walked about on the top of the wold & enjoyed it.

The following day, Anne packed up and 'took the inventory of my books'. On Monday she left for York and the Belcombes. Knowing her predatory reputation, both mothers, first Mrs Belcombe and now Mrs Norcliffe, had to keep an eye on the enthralling Anne Lister.

Mrs Belcombe had five daughters to protect – including a married one, now a Mrs Milne.

Monday 25 Off from Langton at 10 – stopt at Dr Belcombe's at 12 10/"... Went to the minster court – sat 1/2 hour with Mrs & Miss Belcombe – asked Mrs Milne to walk, & we walked 1/2 hour... *But for half a word, she would have been off with me to India – indeed, she said before [ie in front of] her mother, she had not <u>positively</u> declined it.* Mrs Belcombe said Mrs Milne should never have her consent to go with me overland to India...

Off from York at 4 20/"... reached Shibden at 9 35/" – dinner at 10 in the drawing room – sat talking to my aunt.

Back home after her Yorkshire visit and its humiliations, Anne now had a clearer vision of how she would like to improve Shibden. She invested considerable energy in her estate, and even engaged with her father's agricultural concerns. A week earlier, there had

---

[38] VH added that a woman working as a companion would be 'not sufficiently accomplished for a governess – but you have (I suppose) cast off such ideas'.

been local flooding and mud-slides along the far Red Beck bank. She now began to emerge as a dynamically interventionist landowner.

> **Tuesday 26** Walked with my father to Lower brea lane to see the land-slip from Daisy bank into the lane which blocks the road... Spoke to my father about it – promised to make James [Smith] a good road to his house (Well-royde)...
>
> Sauntered about in my walk & up & down & came in at 6 – dinner at 6 10/" – my aunt sat with me at dinner & while I wrote the whole of yesterday & so far of today till 8¼ - then went into the other room to my father & Marian – the newspaper came by John at 9¾ - ½ hour reading it.

Meanwhile, Mariana Lawton, perhaps regretting her coolness towards Anne, breezed past Shibden; Anne managed to take this visit in her stride, confiding to her journal: *'I don't think she quite guesses <u>how much</u> my feelings towards her are calmed & cooled.'*[39]

> **Thursday 28** Walked with M- down my walk & by Well-royde & got to Stump Cross Inn... Saw M- into her carriage & drive off for York... *I walked off, musing for a while in Upper Brea lane, & saying to myself, 'Well, the less I think of & care for her the better.'*

With the Reform Act now law, a general election was imminent. Halifax could now elect two MPs. The Honourable James Stuart Wortley, nephew of Lady Stuart, would stand as the 'blue' (ie Tory) candidate – against a Radical (Stocks) and two Whigs (Rawdon Briggs and Charles Wood). This tough political contest in a new borough in the turbulent industrial north gave Anne a welcome advantage in her correspondence with her southern Tory friends: they needed her news and intelligence for the political survival of their family interest.

Certainly in Halifax, Anne aimed to present herself as the respected owner of ancient Shibden, a member of the influential local gentry, in contrast to the yellow (ie Whiggish) industrialising town. In this, she was assisted by the Listers' friendship with the dignified Waterhouse family of Well-head, who themselves had

---

[39] AL, 27.6.1832.

lived at Shibden Hall in the sixteenth century. Anne considered them, more than any of the other local Tory families, her social equals.[40]

On her visit down into Halifax, Anne, who had a strong loyalty to her servants, first visited her steward who was still very ill.

> **Friday 29** Called & inquired after my steward, Mr James Briggs – 10 minutes there with his poor wife who was in tears – had given up all hope of him. Then called at Well-head – nobody at home – met Mr Waterhouse & walked a little way with him. Stocks has been haranguing his party for two hours today in the assembly room – a radical firebrand sort of speech against present institutions – the honorable James Wortley, Mr Wood, Mr Rawdon Briggs & Stocks [are] candidates for our new borough of Halifax.

> **Saturday 30** Heard at Whitley's [bookshop] that Mr James Stuart Wortley had made a long good speech but [was] so hissed & hooted by the mob as to be hardly audible – Mr Michael Stocks (junior) entreated them to give Mr W- a fair hearing....

> Came to my room at 6₁/2 - till 8 wrote...to Lady S- de R-... 'I am delighted at Vere's prospects of happiness & at all her friends being so satisfied [with the match]... From the 3-fold division among the Whigs [ie with a Radical candidate], I hope Mr James Stuart Wortley has some chance of being brought in for our new borough of H-x – made a good speech this morning in the Piece Hall, but hissed & hooted by the radicals.'

Vere wrote to inform Anne that Donald Cameron had chosen a dark brown carriage, and that Malvern seemed fixed for the marriage journey. It seemed that almost all Anne's friends had husbands. There was virtually nobody left to whom she could

---

[40] They shared her interest in science; for instance, the eldest son, John Waterhouse (b 1806), pursued botany, natural history and geology; he was later elected a Fellow of the Geological Society of London. The Society, formed in 1807, published its first paper by a woman (on earthquakes in Chile) in 1824. However it was not till 1904 that women could be introduced as vistors without the consent of Fellows being required; though in 1909 the Society voted against admitting them as Fellows, and they were not finally admitted till 1919. I am grateful to Sheila Meredith, Chief Librarian, for this information.

confide. She began to feel herself bitterly isolated; and yet, by the etiquette of conventional heterosexual marriage, she *had* to write, however stiltedly, enthusing about the bridegroom's liberality and the bride's happy prospects. Demoralised, she became uncharacteristically indolent and lethargic.

JULY

> **Sunday 1** *It is quite extraordinary how I lie in bed & on the bed – called always at six – this morning & the two before, lay on the bed two hours - & kneeling against it the last three-quarters hour this morning.* Finish dullish morning, F70$\frac{1}{2}$ at 8$\frac{1}{2}$ - read French vocabulary – breakfast with my aunt at 10$\frac{1}{2}$ - then skimmed over last night's courier & walked on the terrace. Prayers & a sermon at 12 in about 50 minutes – then 2 hours in the library reading…& sleeping. From 3$\frac{1}{2}$ to near 6 wrote… to Lady Gordon… 'I wish we could have spent the summer together in Switzerland, & the winter in Italy – there would have been no difficulty in joining forces.'

But, with her steward fatally ill and money limited, Anne could now only just toy with the idea of travelling.

Anne was busy with her tenants and the effects of flooding. (As Anne grew more involved in running the Shibden estate, she became increasingly impatient with her elderly father who would not give up his traditional farming.[41])

She also kept in touch with her old friends, the Priestleys; along with the Waterhouses, she was prepared to consider them almost as social equals.[42] But a coolness now developed in her relationship with William Priestley - which would have unpredictable consequences.

> **Tuesday 3** Off to Lightcliffe… in $\frac{1}{2}$ hour at 9 – breakfast over – [servants] had more tea made for me – Mr Priestley came in & *sat with me a long while, she* [Mrs P-] *was out. Somehow he seemed rather impatient*

---

[41] Eg mowing in Upper Cunnery, AL, 2.7.1832.

[42] William Priestley was an exceptional musical patron; in 1808 he had married Eliza Paley, daughter of Rev William Paley, the eminent theologian, who wrote of God's design in natural phenomena.

or fidgetty to be off to Cliff-hill - tho' I talked of my [estate] concerns... Somehow I never much like Mr P-, I would far rather have his wife – he has the character of liking his own way... I like Mr Waterhouse a thousand times better as a companion (& perhaps for executor)....

Asked Mrs P- to get me a maid if she could... *thinks she (the maid) ought to be able to save five pounds a year – gives her cook fifteen guineas... & gives her housemaid twelve guineas.... She thinks my giving my maid – a thoroughly good one – sixteen pounds a year & a pound on new year's day, enough, with all my cast-off clothes.*

Left Lightcliffe at 1 by my watch... went round by Dumb mill & Lower (& Upper) Place to look at the mischief done at the 2 former 3 weeks ago by the flood....

Went (my aunt & I) into the other room – Marian sat up talking about planting etc till I came to my room at $10_1/2$.

Wednesday 4 *Off with my father to the rent [day], & all the Mytholm [inn] at $11_1/2$... First time in my life of my ever receiving my rents.*

Anne visited elderly Mrs Rawson: Anne's conversation about her own declining social status (not helped by the death of manservant George) was unusually candid. She then took her demoralisation out on poor Throp by cancelling her gardening order.

Thursday 5 Off to H-x at $10_1/4$ - down the old bank to Whitley's to hear the news – Mr Wortley went [ie left] yesterday – sure of his election... Then got to Stoney-royde at $12_1/4$ - dined with Mrs Rawson at $1_1/2$ & came away at 3 – *agreeable visit enough – I thinking Marian is popular there - I said not much about her - but that now I could have neither man nor maid, since George's death – had therefore no conveyance – could not go about, except walking....*

Saw Throp [nurseryman] in the street at H-x, said I could not do the planting I spoke of before quite to [my] mind, & had therefore given it up, & should want nothing of him - at least begged him not to keep either oaks or anything else for me.

However, Shibden's pastoral landscape, with the sound of water running down Red Beck, was always restorative; many of the lush low-lying fields had been named 'Ing', denoting a meadow alongside a stream.

Then a chance social visit occurred that would have major long-term repercussions for Anne.

> **Friday 6** Sauntered about the low land looking at the brook with Pearson[43] & seeing what weaving [ie interlaced twigs] ought to be done[44] – as much as cost a great deal – told him of my intention to lengthen my walk nearly to his bridge over the brook.
>
> Miss [Ann] Walker of Lidgate, & her uncle-in-law & aunt Mr & Mrs Atkinson, called for 1/4 hour at 10 3/4 just as I came in – received them & was very civil – joked Miss W- about travelling – breakfast at 11 5/".

Ann Walker of Lightcliffe, orphaned a decade earlier, was a shy young neighbouring heiress from Lightcliffe, grown even wealthier since the death of her brother in 1830.[45]

Ann and Anne had, of course, met on previous occasions; and – as recently as May – Anne Lister had included Miss Walker in her wish-list to 'get some companion by-and-by'. But on this particular occasion, Anne did not give much more thought to this casual visit. Rather, preoccupied with anxieties and discomforted by constipation, she bent her energies to planting oaks. Then the post brought more unwelcome news.

> **Sunday 8** Read a little of the Courier, & read my letter…from Lady Stuart, Richmond Park – Miss H-'s wedding day not yet fixed, but will probably be the end of this month. 'It would give us <u>both great pleasure</u> if your business does not oblige you to remain [at Shibden], that you, dear Miss Lister, was present at the marriage…. When [the wedding] fixed I will acquaint you, if you feel disposed to come'.
>
> *No, no, she (Miss H-) would as like to have me present as it would suit me to be so. No, no, she will not see <u>me</u> again in a hurry… I know her well enough… She has made no great match of it.*

---

[43] Probably Thomas Pearson of Denmark, whose land ran down to Red Beck.

[44] Probably to improve the under-drainage into Red Beck, using twigs and hedge-cuttings, back-filled with soil.

[45] See *FF*, chap 3 & p 59.

Turning back to home, Anne Lister learnt, by talking to Joseph Stocks, a neighbouring landowner higher up Shibden valley, how he 'has thrown 50 acres into a park-like enclosure and much beautified the head of the dale'; and she also learnt about his small-scale coal-mining – which set her thinking.

Meanwhile, the first post-Reform general election date loomed. With no secret ballot yet, landlords thought it essential to obtain promises from their enfranchised tenants – whose loyalty to the 'blue' cause would be required to ensure Wortley's success in Halifax. Despite her earlier jaundiced conversation with Mrs Norcliffe about politics, Anne Lister had no hesitation in assisting the Tory cause.[46]

> **Thursday 26** Mr [Christopher] Rawson's servant brought me…a note asking me to get John Bottomley's vote for Mr Wortley – went about the matter immediately – [Bottomley] not at home – told his wife to send him to speak to me, saying he must give me his vote…
>
> Said enough this evening to give Washington good hope of being my steward, should anything happen to Briggs.
>
> **Monday 30** Had John Bottomley – sent for him to get his vote for Mr Wortley – he had signed (he said) for Lord Grey & Milton – but I told him the latter would not come forward [as a candidate?], that he, Bottomley, was therefore at liberty & must give me his vote, which he therefore did… Then wrote the following to go early in the morning to 'Christopher Rawson Esquire, Hope hall… 'Dear Sir… John Bottomley says he "signed for Lord Grey & Milton", but, as I told him that Mr Wentworth having declined coming forward, he (Bottomley) was at liberty, he has promised me his vote for Mr Wortley, & you may count upon it – I am, dear sir, very truly yours, A. Lister'. *Then did my clothes for the wash.*
>
> **Tuesday 31** Wrote to Lady S- de R-…congratulations on Miss H-'s marriage today to Donald Cameron Esquire … Never match seemed made with fairer prospects of happiness etc.'

---

[46] However, the majority of AL's tenants lived, not in the urban borough of Halifax, but in the far larger rural county constituency of the West Riding; the latter was not a contested election in 1832, as the Whigs were so dominant.

Anne sent letters in similar vein to Lady Stuart and others. It was at this inauspicious moment that Mariana Lawton happened again to travel through Halifax. It was a fairly low-key visit.

> Told M-, Miss H- was married today to Mr Cameron younger, of Lochiel, but she made no remark – mentioned their going abroad for the winter immediately. Skimmed over the Courier… *Very civil & kind & attentive to M-; in walking home she seemed to take rather more interest about things than she did before – got into bed as soon as I could – not much conversation – she was in pain from her* [inflamed] *ear.*

So July ended, Anne still feeling that she had sunk very low - with not only Mariana but also now with Vere married.

AUGUST

> **Wednesday 1** *A pretty good kiss on getting into bed & another about an hour after, she nothing loth.*[47]… *Lay about an hour talking this morning… She talks of if she sees me at all - but I avoided making any unpleasant remark & all went off well…* Downstairs to breakfast at 11½ in the drawing room, my aunt with us - then just took leave of my father & Marian, & I off with M- in her carriage to H-x at 12½.

Anne was relieved when Mariana drove off from Halifax. It was an intimacy neither woman could finally say goodbye to, but Anne knew that the relationship had little real future.

Then the next day brought double trouble. First Marian and Anne began discussing that most disputatious of subjects: inheritance – and the provisions in Uncle James' 1826 will (which had so favoured Anne at the expense of her younger sister). Tensions were not softened by the increasing divergence in their political views.

> **Thursday 2** Staid talking to Marian….about will-making… she quite set at liberty by my uncle to do whatever she chose with what she

---

[47] Kiss, as well as having its common meaning, was also a euphemism for sexual intercourse.

had[48] – she might leave it to anyone who pleased her in politics... On my quietly saying that, when it came to the point, she would leave what she had, as might be just [ie fair] & not to any political speculator and Cobbett of his day - she said, 'Well! If she had a will to make she should perhaps asterisk [ie omit] everybody'... Marian never shews the smallest intention of leaving anything to me – <u>tout au contraire</u> – that I have no reason to think of leaving her anything...

The <u>Morning Post</u> came, sent 'By order of Mrs Cameron', containing the announcement of her marriage on the 31st ult - at St Martin's church (her parish church at Whitehall) by her uncle, the honorable & reverend dean of Windsor. Then read in the little room with them all...Sharon Turner's [sacred] history of the world before the Deluge.[49]

Controversy over the formation of the Earth before Noah's great flood was a perfect antidote to unpleasant news. Anne Lister, although a keen scientist, was also an observant Anglican, with profoundly conservative social views. [50] Indeed, the Listers (along with the Waterhouses) were of the canal generation, highly suspicious of the new-fangled form of transport – which was unlikely to catch on.

Friday 3 Called at Well-head – all at home... No likelihood of a railroad to oppose us [canal share-holders] during his (Mr W-'s) life – never were more than 3 subscribers in this [Halifax] parish... it would never pay – the Liverpool & Manchester railroad obliged to lower the dividend 1 per cent in consequence of cholera.

The following day, another identical *Morning Post* arrived, sent by Vere Cameron herself, announcing her marriage. Anne retreated

---

[48] Presumably mainly property Marian had inherited from her mother in the East Riding.

[49] Sharon Turner (1768-1847), *The Sacred History of the World: as displayed in the creation and subsequent events to the deluge.*

[50] Among the theorists were the catastrophists (eg the Flood) like Cuvier, and the uniformitarians (gradual processes) like Lyell; debate was both on the likely dating and on the role of God.

into the library, looking at gardening books and reading the newspaper.

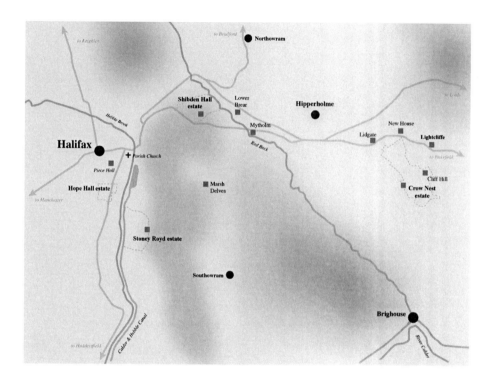

Halifax, Shibden & Lightcliffe
Based on Myers' Map of the Parish of Halifax 1834-35

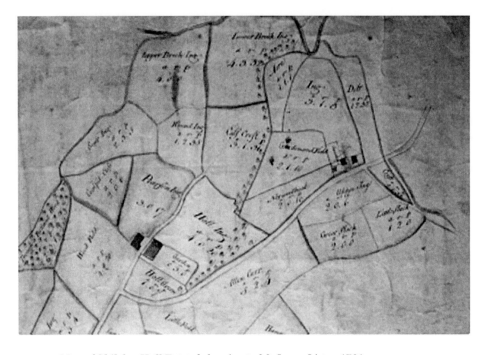

Map of Shibden Hall Estate belonging to Mr James Lister, 1791
SH:2/M/1/2/2 [top part]

Key: A: Daisy Bank B: Tilly Holm C: Lower Brear bridge D: chaumière

B: above 'k' of Lower Brook Ing.

A: to right of B, in middle of Red Beck curve.

C: to right of A, at top of right-hand Red Beck curve.

D: in map, in Lower Brook Ing, under 4.3.3, ie near trees.

This map, drawn the year Anne Lister was born, shows the patchwork of fields (eg Calf Croft) sloping down below Shibden to Red Beck. To the right of Lower Brook Ing is the meandering old curve of the brook; Anne would control the flooding with 'the new cutting', and make the landscape more attractive.

4 THE *CHAUMIÈRE*
10 August – 25 September

Anne had passed four unhappy months since Vere Hobart's proposal; and for three of those months (other than her Yorkshire trip) she had been at Shibden – her first long stay for many years.

With the serious illness of the Shibden steward, Anne Lister was now gaining authority, commanding a small army of men (notably Joseph Pickles) with their carts and horses – which together could move all the earth and stone that her ambitious landscaping plans required.

Meanwhile, Anne visited Mrs Priestley (whose husband William was cousin to Ann Walker); she then called on Ann at her house, Lidgate, nearby. The two women found intimacy in gossiping about common enemies: Marian and a certain Dr Kenny.

> **Friday 10** *About an hour with Pickles in the walk – then at Lightcliffe at 9¾ - sat a couple of hours with Mrs Priestley – glad to see me – thought it above a month since I had been there… Then called on Miss Walker of Lidgate & sat 1¾ hour with her – found her very civil & agreeable. She said… how she disliked Doctor Kenny – as a medical man, he asked queer questions & made odd remarks – she would never have him again. We got on very well together. Thought I, as I have several times done before of late, shall I try & make up to her?*

> Left Miss W- at 1 35/" – a little while in Lower brea wood, clearing trees – then in my walk… Pickles had levelled the walk to beyond the 2nd oak in the arbutus walk [of evergreen shrubs & trees] & begun the weaving.[51]

Anne 'gently advised' Marian 'to fight rather shy of the Kennys', though without hinting why. This hardly helped the two sisters' relationship. Their inheritance squabble was just a tinder-box waiting to ignite. Anne's new assertiveness, with her new 'improvements' at Shibden now taking shape, further inflamed the

---

[51] Here, weaving may mean an interlacing of twigs & branches to thicken a hedge.

situation. Marian retaliated with some Inmans, distant relatives of their mother's.

Sunday 12 Breakfast with my father at 8 20/" – Marian came – long talk with her – *on her leaving me nothing - tho'* [I said] *my uncle's wishes about the Shibden estate were not my fault.... Marian said, [that as] I had said I would not be named with the Inmans, what could she do, if she left them one part & me the other. I said I thought that would be odd enough: I, her sister, & those [Inman] children only cousins-once-removed. 'Well', she [Marian] would marry & hoped to have a child & that would settle all. Begged she would not marry for that... From all she had said, I expected nothing from her - & we would both be alike, both do the same (hinting at my leaving her nothing.) She had said I ought not to have taken [ie inherited] my uncle's property on such conditions.*[52] *...I said I would rather have it on the conditions than not at all.*

My father [Marian claimed] does not like my walk etc; he thinks, with her, I shall not have income to keep these things up. 'I shall find it out', she said, 'by & by'. She expects to be the richest, & that I shall be obliged to sell [Shibden]... These talks always annoy me. Let me name these subjects to her no more.

Tuesday 14 Reading [John] Smith's [English] flora... A dozen large willow stakes come from William Keighley – in my walk – Charles & his son James Howarth made rustic seat (long chair) in my walk [at] bottom of Calf Croft.

Wednesday 15 *Up at a quarter before seven – only little lumps – then again in an hour - & two, about inch & a half long, thick cylinders.... What can be the matter with my bowels? I am not griped [ie pained] at all - in that, these pills do very well.* Fine morning F68$\frac{1}{2}$ at 8 am ...

Went to meet Washington at the brook where he had set out the new cutting... filling up old line [of brook]...

Then (about 12 or before) in my walk – Pickles (& his 2 sons...) weaving &... trenching the arbutus walk – after their dinner they were all employed till night weaving & banking-up the weaving.

Monday 16 From 10 10/" to 1$\frac{3}{4}$ looking over & making extract from

---

[52] Probably that Anne should control the estate on the death of her aunt and father, with nothing for Marian

Turner's sacred history. At 1½ Pickles called & left 2 brace of moorgame... About 7, Pickles called at the door to speak to me – saw he was quite drunk – told him to come tomorrow & bade Rachel[53] shut the door in his face. Made notes from Turner's sacred history.

Though busy with estate work, Anne's plans beyond the boundaries of Shibden were being carefully laid (however casual her explanation to Mrs Priestley). As before, identifying a common enemy provided a very effective way of renewing this acquaintance.

Friday 17 Out at 7½ - first spoke to Pickles (pretty angrily) in the walk – said he must do his job & stick to it or give it up - & not come drunk to speak to me – would soon find this sort of thing would not do for me.

At Lightcliffe at 8¼ - the Priestleys just sitting down to breakfast – breakfasted with them... Some time talking with Mrs P- about Marian – confidential as usual – then she walked with me round the shrubbery.... [I set] off, Mrs P- asking why I went so much sooner than usual – I had said before how late I was.

Called <u>en passant</u> on Miss Walker of Lidgate - & sat with her <u>tête-à-tête</u> from 10 to 1! Talked of household economy - *got on very well – she consulted me about tenant right[54] - & told me all about the Priestleys & really made a too good story against them. He not really a man of business - things went on better without him - & had not (neither he nor Mr Edwards* [the other trustee] *behaved like a gentleman.[55] Said how astonished I was - they (the Priestleys) knew all my family concerns - I meant to leave him my executor - & all she said astonished & grieved me.*

In playing with it, foolishly, broke a pretty ivory, book knife Miss (Catherine) Rawson had given her – very sorry. Miss W- behaved very well about it – [I] said my great consolation was that it would be a good excuse for my giving her one some day from Paris, which I hoped she would value as much as the one destroyed. 'Yes!' She should value it more. *Thought I, 'she little dreams what is in my mind – to*

---

[53] Probably the kitchen maid.

[54] Probably refers to the rights of tenants-at-will.

[55] William Priestley had been appointed co-trustee with Henry Edwards of heiresses Ann and her sister Elizabeth, under the terms of their father's will (1823).

make up to her - she has money and this might make up for rank'. We get on very well so far.

And the thought, as I returned, amused and interested me. She gave me [to take] home with me the last Saturday's penny magazine. Back at my walk at $1_1/2$ & stood there till $6_1/2$ ... Pickles & a new man... began banking up the new part of the walk in Tilly holm...

Home at $6_3/4$ - some time in the little room – my aunt had been uneasy at my being out all [day] & nobody knowing where I was.

But, rather than Anne planning an immediate repeat visit to Lidgate, nothing happened. Instead, she remained immersed in her practical landscaping activity down by Red Beck. It was almost as if she was coolly allowing this unexpected re-acquaintance to mulch down while she mused over its full romantic and economic potential - and how exactly to 'make up to' shy Ann Walker.

Meanwhile, the two sisters continued to wrangle over the inequitable provisions in Uncle James' will. This time, they quarrelled in front of their father (who turned a deaf ear). Why, for instance, had Uncle James left Shibden to his niece and not to his brother?

Saturday 18 Breakfast at 8 20/" with my father & Marian in $1/2$ hour – some observation about the house made me say 'Well! But my father must keep it in repair.' 'No!' said Marian... [I] said that would not do [as an argument] – I had never cost my father anything... 'Well! But', said Marian, 'my uncle left you all he had'. 'Yes!' [I replied] '& if he had not, my father must have done [ie paid] all for me'. 'Well! He would have had [ie owned] the estate'... She takes a bad way to mend matters...

In 25 minutes read over Miss Walker's penny magazine of last Saturday – well enough, but not worth much time in reading. Out at $1_3/4$, having been some time with my aunt – found Pickles & 2 men & 1 boy at the [em]bankment & digging for weaving up to the Tilly-holm bridge...

Talked to my aunt – said how long I had sat with Miss Walker yesterday – what she had said had almost inclined me to put [ie think] the Priestleys in the wrong.

Monday 20 Out at 6 35/" – with Pickles beginning the weaving at

Tilly-holme bridge – 1/2 hour in library reading over what I read of Thucydides yesterday… Charles H- & James put me down willow stakes this morning in my walk against the brook.

Anne also hoped to build a small but attractive garden hut on the lower Shibden slopes, with a vista over Red Beck. From such plans, a scheme was forming in her mind that would draw together so many of the key threads of her life since she had left Hastings. It remained in her semi-consciousness, hardly surfacing yet in her own diary, even in its secret coded passages.

Rather, she gave immediate vent to the full details of her highly ambitious plans to remodel the house interior. It was almost as if she had determined to stamp her mark on Shibden, making it distinctly *hers* rather than Marian's.

> **Thursday 23** Charles [H-] cut down the oak next [to] the 2 beeches in the walk, & cut it up for the little hut I am going to put up, near the lily bank, or rather at the entrance of the Lower brook Ing wood…
>
> Sat up talking to my aunt (how to alter the house) till 11 1/2 - the best idea I have ever had yet – to turn the hall into the kitchen – drawing-room (front half) into housekeeper's room…my aunt as she is – blue room stairs up the green room way…
>
> I will immediately set about <u>righting</u> the present stick heap & planting ivy against that end of the house so that it may be covered & look more decent by the time I want to make the above temporary alterations, which will suffice till I am rich enough to do more.

Although Anne's immediate improvements were very modest, in them lie the beginnings of what would begin to transform Shibden.

> **Friday 24** Breakfast at 8 10/" with my father in 1/2 hour – told him of tidying the stick heap – building a low wall against the house (against the cattle) & planting the latter with ivy – [he] did not appear to like it much but said nothing absolutely against it…
>
> Then again in the walk, with Pickles preparing foundation of my <u>chaumière,</u> & afterwards planted out 5 hollies on embankment at the low end of the walk – he was weaving till about (before) 11. I myself went to my own quarry at 10, & got George [Naylor's] cart (leading [ie carrying] weaving stuff for Pickles) to bring me down a load of

heavy stuff [ie stone] for foundation of <u>chaumière</u> – so heavy, 1/2 hour in loading.

Almost overnight Anne's 'little hut' had become transformed into a more elegant-sounding *chaumière*, a small thatched cottage. However, her diary provides no indication of the origin of the inspiration for the *chaumière* (or, as she later called it, moss-house).[56] What is clear is that she intended it to be a private space, a female refuge.[57]

> **Saturday 25** Went down to Charles H- & his son James, putting up the <u>charpente</u> [framework] of the <u>chaumière</u> - perhaps I shall thatch it with moss & call it the moss-house.
>
> **Sunday 26** Went down to my aunt at 11 1/2 - poorly again - amused her by talking of altering the house – better idea than what seemed to me the best on Thursday – to... turn the upper kitchen into cooking kitchen – my aunt's present bedroom into back kitchen[58] – Hemingway's room into butler's pantry – hall into dining-room....
>
> At 12 5/" read the morning service, sermon 7 [by] Mr Knight[59] in exactly 50 minutes, as I generally do. Then looking about – true, the house is not worth much altering – should do little [to improve it] or pull it down at once.

This idea was a little drastic (luckily, the house was not pulled down). But Anne certainly felt oppressed by her immediate family

---

[56] It may have been inspired by AL's French travels; from a garden she had visited in Britain; from contemporary horticultural journalism; or from a landscape book (eg in Shibden library).

[57] Thanks to Professor Bill Stafford & his seminar on 'The Gender of the Place'. The location suggests that neither Marian nor their father ventured to this lower part of the estate, lying between SH & Lightcliffe.

[58] Probably moved downstairs because of her spasms etc.

[59] Rev Samuel Knight was the late Vicar of Halifax; his sermon VII was on 'The Omniscience of God'

and by the shabby inconvenience of Shibden.[60]Then a letter arrived from Vere Cameron in Brussels, bubbling with happiness: they were going to Turin, and might see Anne in Rome or Naples in the winter.

> **Monday 27** Cut down 2 small oaks in James Smith's (Well-royde) hedge... & 4 ditto from the hedge dividing Calf-croft & Upper Brook Ing – so that the <u>chaumière</u> has nine small oaks & a couple of large torn oak branches.

Then, as she planned her return visit to Lightcliffe, Anne's sense of anticipation and impatience grew. She still had the indignity of having to walk wherever she went but as she walked, she learnt. Given the current radical agitation, even sophisticated Anne Lister remained gullible to lurid stories of impending industrial insurrection.

> **Thursday 30** *Mending the bottom of pelisse* – read five or 6 pages of French vocabulary & breakfast at 7³/₄, to give me time to go soon to Lightcliffe – breakfast with my father... Out at 8 50/″ – had only just got to the gate when driven back by rain – did a little more vocabulary. Hinchcliffe (of Lightcliffe) came about 9₁/₄ & staid an hour – came about the few coals I had left...
>
> Raining hard – no chance of Lightcliffe today... Such a cold air blowing round my loins from between door & window, obliged to wrap my great-coat round me & throw my tartan cloak across my knees.
>
> Out at 4 35/″ – along the walk – along the brook to Lower brea bridge, then to Charles H-'s shop... 3 millions of men in unions - & a delver told Charles they [had] 28 bushels of gold, so should not be starved if the masters would not raise the wages & they (the men) were out of work.

At a time when women were excluded from formal higher education and from the learned professional societies, women

---

[60] Her constipation did not help: she wrote a long and despairing letter ('intestinal torpor') to Dr Belcombe, seeking help.

scientists like Anne Lister were disadvantaged when engaging with the swirling intellectual debate between geology and theology. [61]

> **Friday 31** From 7 25/" to 8 5/" made several notes & read from p 231 to 259... of 'Reliquiae Diluvianae, or observations on the Organic Remains contained in caves, fissures, & diluvial [ie of Noah's Flood] gravel, & on other geological phenomena, attesting [to] the action of an universal deluge', 1823, by the reverend William Buckland BD, FRS, FLS, member of the geological society of London etc etc, & professor of min-eralogy & geology in the university of Oxford....[62]

> Breakfast at 8₁/₄ with my father in 25 minutes – out at 8₃/₄ - met Jonathan Mallinson at Whitehall – told him he must give up having the masons & delvers fortnightly union meetings at his house, or they would stamp [ie trample] it down – besides, these meetings were not respectable & he would have his license taken from him.

Meanwhile, also in Lightcliffe, Mrs Priestley remained a good source of advice both about the choice of suitable creepers and on finding a Scottish servant. About Ann Walker, it was in Mrs Priestley that Anne had to confide. Although she was not the orphaned heiress's mother (and so not like Mrs Norcliffe or Mrs Belcombe), Mrs Priestley was still probably the most appropriate woman to act *in loco parentis*. However, Anne could always cleverly manipulate situations; and here she artlessly conveyed to her old confidante the impression that she still had not identified 'a fixed companion'.

> At Lidgate in 35 minutes at 9 20/" – Miss Walker at home – sat with her near a couple of hours, then proposed going to Cliff-hill – we sat 35 minutes with Miss [aunt] Walker, & then, after having sauntered & looked about, both before & after our call, I left Miss W- junior at her

---

[61] Polly Salter, *The Scientific Life of a Genteel Yorkshire Woman*, research essay, Leeds University, 2000, compared AL with Mary Somerville & Caroline Herschel, unable to present their own findings to the Royal Society, & did not become honorary fellows until 1835; associative membership was usually experienced vicari-ously through their closest male relative, which put AL at a double disadvantage.

[62] William Buckland (1784-1856), was a catastrophist; Lyell had attended his lectures on mineralogy at Oxford

own gate about 1 & went to Lightcliffe.

Mrs P- not at home, but found her at her school & sat about a couple of hours with her – got her to tell me what creepers to have for my <u>chaumière</u>. Said how well Miss W- & I got on together – had been at Cliff-hill together – asked her...to enquire for a Highland servant for me. Then got on to grave subjects – [I was] more unsettled than ever since... All my thoughts of a fixed companion frustrated – must have someone – difficult to choose again.... *She mentioned Mrs Lawton – 'Oh, no, I liked her very much, but that was a different thing' - & made the same answer about Miss [Isabella] Norcliffe. All this was to throw Mrs P- off the thought of M-, whom I know she must have fancied I had fixed on.*

I got on as usual - friendly as ever – tho' at first it struck me, [what] she thought of my seeing so much of Miss Walker? Perhaps the Priestleys will think of it by & by.

Miss W- & I do certainly get on marvellously – she seems quite confidential & glad to see me – told me of her plans of altering the Cliff-hill grounds etc. Miss Walker & I talked of her going with Miss (Catherine) Rawson to Wastwater lake on Wednesday... Said she would like to see the giant's causeway & lake of Killarney – so should I – said I would take her next month, & she would have gone but for having promised to go to Wastwater! I hoped she would not be long away – to be back before the end of next month – she would like well enough to see Switzerland – shall I get her there? *Mentioned my being lost near Wastwater, & begged her to think of me there. <u>'Yes' she should not forget me.</u> Really, I almost think she has no dislike to me, at any rate - who knows how it may end - I shall be wary this time.* Miss W- likely enough to get me a Highland man-servant. In short, I shall really be glad enough when she is come back again...

Then went with Charles & James H-... & cut 7 or 8 small oaks to finish the <u>chaumière</u> & make door for it etc.

September 1832

Anne Lister spent time on anxious preparations, hiding signs of Shibden's shabbiness, for a formal round of calls on the families of the Halifax élite – in Ann Walker's carriage. And, as Anne Lister was increasingly aware, they were so often Ann Walker's relatives[63] – like the Edwards of Pye-nest, the other side of Halifax.

So September marked the start of a possible new life for Anne Lister. Would this new relationship really meet her desires for both love and for fortune? Her diary entries record both her anxiety *and* her worldly-wise cynicism.

> **Saturday 1** Charles & James H- at the <u>chaumière</u>... Pickles finished the culvert in the morning & in the afternoon planted out 3 or 4 little hollies on the bank opposite the <u>chaumière</u>, & removed from there the 2 yews & 1 Portugese laurel to behind the <u>chaumière</u>,... & dressed [prob: straightened] off walk below the <u>chaumière</u> to the brook.

> **Sunday 2** *Mending my stockings.* Breakfast 8 35/" - Marian soon came & kept me talking politics till 9 55/"... Wrote...to I. N-... 'Thanks for the congratulations on my friend's marriage - never match seemed made under better auspices - everybody pleased - we were all to meet this winter; but I know not as yet how far I shall be able to keep to these plans - I see no chance of getting off from here on this side [of] Xmas - I have never had more business on my hands...'

> Read aloud the morning service & sermon (8) Mr Knight. Read over last night's paper - came upstairs at 13/4. *Till three & a half sewing watch-pocket in new pelisse & putting strings to petticoat & getting all ready to put on tomorrow to go with Miss Walker.* Went out at 3 35/" - long while walking on the terrace with my father & Marian, then loitering in the garden till dinner.

> **Monday 3** Letter (3 pages, hurried) from M-... sadly harassed - had for-gotten her writing desk...[64]

> Put on my new pelisse, 1st time, & off with Miss Walker, who had been sitting 1/4 hour with my aunt, at 11 50/". We... drove to Pyenest - 1/2 hour there... Then 3/4 hour at Throp's - looking at shrubs & flowers - then called at the door, each left own card, & particularly inquired after Mrs Saltmarshe - & then made sundry shoppings, &

---

[63] Interestingly, AL does not comment in her diary about this seemingly threatening information.

[64] Their correspondence often now concerned finding suitable servants. M- was probably experiencing the menopause.

Miss W- set me down at our own gate at 5 1/2.

Changed my dress in 10 minutes & went down into the walk.... William Green drove the cart...

Dinner at 6 1/2 - afterwards... sent off (at 8), 3 pages to Mrs Lawton... nothing particular... said I had written to her brother – he was very kind...but had had no time to take medicine as yet.[65]

Miss W & I got on very well - she was not for going to Pye-nest - showed me a queer huffy letter she had had from Mrs Edwards[66] - would not call before November - I advised differently & we went - but I see there will be no cordiality again between them - this will not suit me the less well. She seems well enough inclined to consult me & tell me all - I am to choose shrubs for her & she for me.

I begged her not to stay [away] longer than three weeks or, if she did, not [to] go so soon as Wednesday, to be back on the twenty-sixth, & I would breakfast with her on the twenty-seventh - at which she seemed pleased. Joked & said she had better go with me & be at Rome for Easter - her refusal was weak enough to make me guess her going as possible - she does not seem to dislike me, at any rate. Well, what shall we make of it? If she was fond of me & manageable, I think I could be comfortable enough with her.

Wrote the above of today till 8 1/2. Miss Walker left me today the 3 (8vo) volumes History of Paris I saw & asked for when last calling on her (on Friday) - read a few pages vol 1 History of Paris - asleep a little while.... Began harvest (cutting oats in the Hanging hey) this morning.

During Ann Walker's visit to the Lakes, Anne Lister grew almost obsessive about the estate detail she recorded in her diary: barrowing soil, replanting a holly hedge, carting stone – all back-breaking work still undertaken by local men and cart-horses.[67]

Tuesday 4 Pickles & his son George & William Greenwood raising the walk from the willows to the great ash... After dinner read over

---

[65] Dr Steph Belcombe had helped AL with her constipation.

[66] Wife of AW's mother's brother, Henry Edwards; she was also a cousin of William Priestley.

[67] Shibden had cart-horses, including one called Ball

Marian's <u>Gardener's Magazine</u> no 15 (for this month).[68]

Wednesday 5 *Incurred a cross thinking of Miss Walker - first time - fine morning F63o at 7 5/" - mended pelisse.* Breakfast with my father at 81/4... Went to my aunt, at or before 9 - better but weak & poorly - out again at 9 10/" - all the day in the walk...

Pickles & his sons John & Robert finished dressing up the walk & moved Portugese laurel from the front to the upper side of the chaumière.... Dick & William Greenwood... got up earth from along the holly hedge in Lower brook Ing & barrowed it to the slope in front of the <u>chaumière</u>.

Thursday 6 Pickles dug over the east slope from the oak nearest the <u>chaumière</u> ... William G- helped David to thatch the hut in the afternoon... David the thatcher brought his son (quite a boy) with him at 2 25/" & got on making one side of the thatch of the <u>chaumière</u> or hut - done with rushes...

Very kind letter from Lady Stuart... tells me his majesty had granted to Vere & her sisters [permission?] to take the rank of earl's daughters - so my friend is now my Lady Vere Cameron - well! I am very glad of it - all parties will be pleased.

Anne had little option but to sound sweetly civilised about this, but it must have been doubly galling to learn that Vere Cameron was to join the aristocracy.

Friday 7 *Incurred a cross last night thinking of Miss Walker...* Breakfast at 9 in 1/2 hour with Marian...[69] Out again at 101/2 - in the walk all the day - the calves had got in last night & some cows & done for too much damage – cropt [cropped] to destruction my fine young lime tree & a fine arbutus, & several (a great many) young oaks, & did damage to a Portugese laurel, rhododendrons etc - sadly vexed about it...[70] George P - brought a load of rushes - told Pickles not to tell

---

[68] *Gardener's Magazine*, edited by John Claudius Loudon, 1826-34.

[69] They discussed kitchens and cooking. It seemed that Elizabeth Cordingley cooked the family meals in the hot cooking (lower) kitchen; and AL's meal was to be cooked separately in the upper kitchen.

[70] AL had tried to secure the area by her walk as animal-free; she had a gate at the bottom of Calf Croft to stop the cows roaming in again.

David the thatcher to come again - thought John could do it better - if not, Pickles to do it himself - would have it twice as thick laid on. Charles H- had told me the wind would soon blow it off as it is. [71]

Dinner at 71/4 - my aunt with me - better this evening. Wrote the whole of the above of today - found Loudon's 'Gardener's dictionary', [72] & nice civil kind note from Miss Walker - she goes on Monday with Miss Catherine Rawson - to sleep that night at Bowness & the next (Tuesday) at Keswick & then (she says) see 7 lakes before getting to Wastdale. *I think we shall get on together - she feels satisfied at having called at Pye-nest & grateful to me for persuading her to do so. I wonder if I can at all mould her to my own way.*

My aunt left me at 83/4... looked at the courier - Marian staid talking - then talking to my aunt *about my little care for M-*. Came upstairs at 103/4 ... about an hour looking into <u>Loudon's Encyclopaedia of gardening</u>

What could be more appropriate gift-exchange between two landed women than a gardening book, illustrated with wood-engravings, by popular writer John Claudius Loudon? And, from the bottom of her walk, Anne Lister was part-way to Lightcliffe already.

Saturday 8 *Brushing pelisse & petticoat near half hour* - fine foggyish morning F63° at 63/4, breakfast at 8 5/" in 40 minutes with my father, & out at 8 50/", in the walk till 9 50/". Then walked to Lidgate in 1/4 hour. 10 minutes with Miss Walker, going off to Huddersfield at 12 - thanked her for her note & Loudon - *very good friends. Then* went to the Priestleys' & sat 11/2 hour with her...

Returned by Lower Brea - back in the walk at 12 10/" - remained there till home at 63/4. ... Charles & James H- all the day thatching north side of the hut, George P- brought a load of rushes...

Jameson's mineralogy (3 volumes, Miss Walker's) sent up to me from

[71] Charles Howarth was a practical man for whom thatched cottages doubtless seemed the effete indulgences of the eccentric gentry.

[72] Probably John Claudius Loudon, *Encyclopedia of Gardening; comprising the theory and practice of horticulture...including... a General History of Gardening in All Countries,* 1822, updated 5ᵗ edition 1828.

Whitley's [bookshop in Halifax] this afternoon – after dinner read the first 136 pages of introduction & the first 6 pages of the work itself. Went into the other room at 9 40/"... some time at Italian grammar (Biagoli).

Anne Lister continued corresponding with her élite friends in the south. Her news was of Owenite trade union ferment. Anne was probably genuinely fearful of the threat of class consciousness, but she also cleverly talked up the local dangers. Among the women she wrote to was Lady Vere Cameron; she still had to pretend delighted congratulations, and added:

> **Sunday 9** Mention my aunt's being so much worse than usual lately that I could not leave her unless better - otherwise had intended being off the middle or end of January...& being at Rome for the carnival...[73] Politics - bad prospect for the winter - expect the mill I have spent so much upon will hardly be allowed to stand over it [ie over winter].[74] A fearful number of people have turned out for increase of wages - the different trades have their respective unions; & each member admitted binds himself by a solemn and dreadful oath to obey their "officers" in every-thing, even in murdering a <u>bad master</u>. They hold weekly meetings in large rooms which they allow no one to enter while they are there; & all that transpires is, that they make a noise as if they were at a military drill, that 40 and 50 pistol shots and more are commonly fired off in one night - a pistol is fired over every man's head immediately on his taking the oath, so that the number of shots tells the number of new members - they vow vengeance against machinery[75] - & I expect the mill will not be allowed to stand'. Reform bill hardly mentioned... Wish we may get off as quietly over the winter here as I trust they [the Camerons] will in Italy.

---

[73] If AL hoped that VC would be an intimate friend, it was probably a forlorn hope by now.

[74] Probably George Robinson's wire mill at Mytholm; again, she may be exaggerating her investment in it.

[75] The memory of the Luddites nearby in the West Riding was still very real.

Meanwhile Anne 'planned bringing up path (to join my walk) to the upper garden door', and she organised the thatching of the 'west end & 2 sides' of the 'hut'. It was fairly elaborate, with a proper floor, a 'lift-up bench & part of table' and a properly-hung door.[76]

Anne's own reading included Ann Walker's copy of Jameson's 'mineralogy' - partly because she was beginning to value Shibden's own mineral wealth; partly because of the current intellectual debates; and partly because she had her own mineral collection, and was no slouch when it came to a critical reading of science.

> **Sunday 16** Looking over Swiss minerals - breakfast with my father at 8 20/"... From 12 in 50 minutes read prayers & sermon (9) Mr Knight.[77] Meant to have gone out into my walk immediately, but sat down at the desk & from 1 to 4 50/", wrote out sinopsis of ... [a] system of mineralogy... The 4 classes of Jameson, divided into earthy, saline, metalliferous & inflammable minerals, & then subdivided into orders, which, giving no hint at the composition of the mineral, would never make the deepest possible impression on a mind constituted like mine - though there is much in Jameson which makes me determined to have his work - excellent for synonyms & derivations.
>
> Ran out for 3/4 hour at 5 10/" to the end of my walk & returned leisurely. Dinner at 7¼ - my aunt, having been sick on sitting down to dinner with my father & Marian, had veal soup & rice pudding with me. Read the first 23 pages Loudon's gardener's encyclopaedia.
>
> **Monday 17** A little while with my aunt - better this morning, but looks ill - came to my room at 11 40/" & till 2 looking at my minerals in the little box - 36 specimens good, & the 80 ditto (not well named & not therefore of much use & too many granites) from Chamonix that I. N- sent me from there.... Came upstairs at 10 - looking over Jameson's mineralogy till near 11.
>
> **Marginalia**: my steward, Mr James Briggs, died about 10 this evening

[76] AL, 13, 14 & 15.9.1832; it seemed to have fold-away garden furniture. The 'upper garden door' was perhaps at the corner of Hall Green, fairly near the house.

[77] Proverbs iii 6, 'in all thy ways acknowledge Him, and He shall direct thy paths'.

of dropsy, having been severely ill & confined chiefly to his room since about the middle of June last, leaving his widow & 1 unmarried daughter slenderly provided for.

Tuesday 18 With Pickles channelling - home again at 12 – heard a company rap [knock] – got into the hall chamber[78] & sat quietly there till all inquiries for me had passed away - then slunk out, & Booth & nobody knew where I had been - would have made my appearance had I known it was Mr & Mrs William Priestley that called.

Wednesday 19 A little while looking into De la Beche's geology - out at 7¼ - in the walk... George Pickles brought the 2nd 20 sacks of moss – chaining & training brambles near my rustic chair, & pruning spanish nut-trees & 2 or 3 little oaks till after 6.... Read ½ dozen pages Loudon's Encyclopedia of Gardening to p 29 - went into the little room at 9 35/'" - stayed talking to Marian - came to my room at 10¾.

With the 'hut' now finished, Anne Lister could enjoy her leisure in this, her own private world. She had made it into a civilised and secluded mossed summer-house.

Thursday 20 *Incurred a cross thinking of Miss Walker just before getting up....* Went up with Pickles (on his leaving work at 5¾) to set out the addition to the walk to bring it into the garden at the upper door, & staid in the hut reading yesterday's paper, which Martha Booth brought to me in the walk between 11 & 12 this morning, having gone on purpose to H-x for it.

Dinner at 7 – afterwards read p 29 to 49 Loudon's Encyclopedia of Gardening – very interesting – p 30 article 141 mentions the botanical garden of M. Parmentier... Les dames Girardin walked about their garden at Ermenonville in "common brown stuff, en amazones, with black hats".[79]

---

[78] Rooms above the Hall; AL subsequently opened up the Hall, removing this storage space

[79] The hermitage at Ermenonville, built c 1775 by the Marquis de Giradin, had a conical thatched roof; Rousseau visited shortly before he died.

With weaving developed at Tilly-holme bridge, Anne's walk now extended no less than half a mile, 'from the house door to the Tilly-holme gate'.[80]

> **Saturday 22** Charles & James H- mossed the front [of the hut] & just the top of the north side in the morning....
>
> Holdsworth, who has Mr Rawson's quarry,... speaking of coals, said Rawsons employed 40 men... they had a good trade of it - but as soon as the delvers get their wages advanced, the colliers mean to turn out for an advance.

With her aunt remaining very ill, Anne wanted to convert the north parlour into a bedroom for her.

> **Sunday 23** Fine morning F59° at 6.10 - brushing pelisse etc etc - out at 7 25/" - mainly sauntering about the house - breakfast with my father at 8 - thinks he would consent to have the north parlour fitted up for my aunt - stood talking with him or Marian - took the latter to see the bit of walk from the upper garden door to the Hall-wood gate... Then had my aunt in the north parlour, & afterwards looked about - found it would be a <u>strongish</u> job - told both my father & Marian so, & that if my aunt was not anxious about it I would give it up....
>
> George Robinson came at 6 40/"... [his mill] got 17 orders (opened 17 accounts) in Scotland, but [he] means now to stay at home...has got a traveller to whom he is to pay on commission.
>
> **Monday 24** Dick made drain from the old dry bridge across the new part of the walk... Charles H- & George P- went with Pickles' cart for rushes ... [I] read last night's courier in the hut.

Anne had also corresponded with Mariana Lawton about a possible *femme de chambre*, Eugénie Pierre. [81]

> **Tuesday 25** Out at 7 20/" at the hut – with Dick doing the continuation of the walk from the Hall-wood gate[82] – Charles & James

---

[80] AL, 21.9.1832.

[81] Lady's maid – with none of the tricky social blurring of a *dame de compagnie*

[82] Probably a gate out from wooded Hall Ing onto the road above SH, The 'old dry bridge' was probably nearby.

H- set the new gate there. Breakfast at 10₁/₄ in the drawing room – my aunt soon came… [I had] given up all thought of doing anything at the north parlour and north chamber at present - had had a new idea & the best on the subject that had occurred to me yet – would move the hall stairs altogether & turn them up the little upper buttery…

Out again at 11₃/₄ - chiefly with Dick & Charles H-, then went down to the weaving to see what Pickles was about - found him doing the new cut between Pearson's sown holm & Mallinson's Ing.[83] Went to the Stag's Head to ask if they had had, & why they had, more union meetings of the delvers there – Mrs Mallinson said her husband did not understand about it - I said I had told him as plain as I could speak, I would not have them at the Mytholm [inn], & if he did not understand now, I should take some other means of making him understand - he must make up his mind to give up these meetings or leave the house….

Letter… from M-…she enclosed a letter from Mlle Pierre,… Eugénie's sister, & says… From Mlle Pierre's account Eugénie is likely enough to suit me - she will travel outside [the coach], and tho' M- told her I should not want her till January, [she] does not seem inclined to give up all hope of my place - her health good, & she wishes to travel… *Her [M-'s] letter seems as if she thought of me affectionately - does she half-repent the break between us? Heaven only knows. If I can get Miss Walker, she will be surprised - she talks of my probably settling abroad for some years.* M- would not advise me to take a foreigner if I was going to remain at home, but on my return advises me to 'take a steady respectable woman who you can depend upon to look after your other servants'. *This seems as if she had no thought of ever being with me.*

---

[83] Probably between the fields below Denmark & the Stag's Head, Mytholm.

5. AS GOOD AS A MARRIAGE

In the Moss House: 26 September - 25 October

With the return of Ann Walker from the Lakes, the emotional tenor of Anne Lister's days once again shifted. Books became less intellectual stimulation and more symbolic gift-exchange, cementing their fast-developing relationship. Anne might be the more scholarly of the two, but it was Ann Walker who could run up book-shop bills – and then lend these new volumes to Anne.

> **Wednesday 26** *Incurred a cross thinking of Miss Walker...* Out at 10¹/₄ - some time with the workmen, and saw Washington at the weaving. Then called at Lightcliffe - Mrs Priestley out - then called to inquire if Miss Walker was returned - yes! last night.

> Sat with her from 12 50/" to 2 20/" - she had brought me a <u>presse-papier</u> [paper-weight] from the marble works at Kendal. *Very civil - our conversation quite confidential & we really get on very well - yet she said she could not go to Italy. They give old Washington [as steward] seventy pounds a year & young ditto the same - for the management of the property....*

> Then with the workmen & did not come in till 5 20/" - went in to my aunt - found Miss Walker's servant had been for her books - came upstairs & wrote a note to go with them by John tonight...: 'Ten thousand apologies' - know what a disappointment that sort of thing is about books - sorry & annoyed – thanks – 'may I keep [History of] <u>Paris</u> a little longer? ... I find myself very busy [on the estate] on my return from having played truant so unexpectedly long with you - besides, you always give me so much to think of afterwards, that it is long after I have actually left you, before my mind seems disengaged.... Do pray forgive me before morning' - Jameson, [vol] ii, [page] 493, Ancient or antique marbles. 'May I beg for my <u>press-paper</u>- now that you have given it me, I am impatient to have it - very truly yours, A Lister'.

> Sent off this note... by John at 7¹/₂ with the books & bill, Jameson, 3 vols (8vo Edition 3, Edinburgh 1820 50/-), and Loudon's <u>Encyclopedia of Gardening</u> (edition 5ᵗʰ, London 1828, very large thick 8vo, 40/), and James's Sunday school teacher's guide (ed. 12, London 1830, 2/-) that I

have never looked into - read to p 83 (vol 3) Jameson, & to p. 61 Loudon.

Dinner at 7¹/₄ in ¹/₂ hour… All the corn got in this morning - Dick working for me today - widening the new walk done yesterday & getting on & spreading ashes.

Anne Lister could exercise smooth dexterity when it came to the etiquette of the loan and return of books. She knew all about courtly for-malities, about 'making myself agreeable' - and making the most of new private architectural spaces and pastoral vistas.

Thursday 27 Fine morning tho' hazy - F70o at 6 - off to Lidgate at 7¹/₂ - along the high road & at Lidgate at 8 - Miss Walker ready to see me, & breakfast almost immediately - sat talking about an hour over the breakfast table then adjourned to the other [room], & were just going out about 12¹/₂ when Mrs Stansfield & Miss Delia Rawson called (from Gledholt near Huddersfield, 7 miles off) & stayed an hour. Miss W- glad I had sat them out - dined with her at 2, & at 3¹/₄ we were off for her to see my walk.

Walked slowly by the new road & Lower brea, & sauntered to nearly the Hall-wood gate in my walk - then on returning rested in the hut & must have sat there a couple of hours. Walked home with her at 5 50/" in 40 minutes & back in ¹/₂ hour or less, at 2 or 3 minutes before 7….

Dinner at 7 00/" - my aunt with me - sat talking to her till she left near 9 - then wrote the above of today. *Miss W- & I very cozy & confidential - on parting, she said she knew not when she had spent so pleasant a day - I believe her - she sat & sat in the moss house, hardly liking to move. Of course I made myself agreeable, & I think she already likes me even more than she herself is aware. She seemed pleased at my reminding her of our walk ten years ago by Hill-top [Lightcliffe] etc - when I had joked about her going abroad - said it had always been my intention to make the offer more seriously as soon as I could - that she must remember I had always been in the same strain - that I had never joked anyone else in the same way, & I hoped she would now understand that I was more serious than she supposed. She said her uncle & aunt Atkinson had said I should get her abroad - but that she had told them 'Oh no, it was all joke'. 'Ah', said I, 'then they understood me better than you did'. She had told me before that she was always told I was not to be depended on - I success-fully parried this & she believes me.*

We talked of the Priestleys etc - I dextrously giving her to understand that she would turn me [ie my opinion] quite. I consulted with her in all frankness of confidence what I should [do] about the French maid etc. Talked to her about planting trees at Shibden etc etc.- said how much good change of climate would do her - & I now really believe she will go with me! She seems to take all I say for gospel... & in fact she seems inclined to follow my advice implicitly - she consults me about her affairs.

Said she was sure people never meant us to get together - that Mrs Stansfield Rawson looked odd on finding me there - & in short we congratulated ourselves that chance & Doctor Kenny (I always thank her for the kindness of telling me the plot to catch [ie capture] Marian) had made us better acquainted. She said she would call on my aunt on Monday - I to meet her between nine & ten. I really did feel rather in love with her in the hut, & as we returned. I shall pay due court for the next few months - & after all, I really think I can make her happy & myself too.

'Well', said I to myself as I left her, 'She is more in for it than she thinks - she likes me certainly'. We laughed at the idea of the talk our going abroad together would [stir]. She said it would be as good as marriage. 'Yes', said [I], 'quite as good or better'. She falls into my views of things admirably. I believe I shall succeed with her - if I do, I will really try to make her happy - & I shall be thankful to heaven for the mercy of bringing me home, having first saved me from Vere, rid me of M-, & set me at liberty.

We shall have money enough. She will look up to me & soon feel attached & I, after all my turmoils, shall be steady &, if God so wills it, happy. If Vere had rank & was more charming, she would have always thought she did me a favour [84] - & M- has annoyed me too often. I can gently mould Miss W- to my wishes - & may we not be happy? How strange the fate of things! If after all, my companion for life should be Miss Walker - she was nine-and-twenty a little while ago! How little my aunt or anyone suspects what I am about! Nor shall it be surmised till all is settled.

Had just written the above at near 10 - 3/4 hour in the little room & came upstairs at 10 1/4. Pickles & co at the weaving.

The relationship would be 'as good as marriage... quite as good or better'. Anne Lister had an edge of worldly cynicism towards 'the

---

[84] Of course, in reality it was no longer if Vere had rank, but rather now that Vere <u>did</u> have rank

victory to be won' with Ann Walker. Anne would *'like her quite well enough for comfort'*, and the intimacy in all its rich complexities now accelerated fast.

> **Friday 28** Breakfast with my father at 8 in 35 minutes. *Musing before getting up & as I dressed of Miss Walker - I think we should be happy together - I should gently lead her into my own ways & soon be really attached to her - to the exclusion of all care for anyone else...*

> Out in the walk at 10 - pruning young oaks till 2 - from 2 to 3 10/" asleep in the hut *or rather the last twenty five minutes incurred a cross thinking of Miss Walker - I shall think myself into being in love with her - I am already persuaded I like her quite well enough for comfort.*

> Home at 3$_{1/2}$ meaning to write letters - talking for 2 or 3 minutes to Marian - when company rap [knock] at the door, & Miss Walker shewn into the drawing room - her call seemed to be on my aunt – sat about 1/2 hour, & I then walked back with her down the walk. She asked if I had got her note - no! then explained that she had come to ask my advice about her tenant (Collins) having forced open the barn door opening into her court yard.

> This matter settled, we sat down in the hut for about 3/4 hour till 5 50/". I then walked with her to her own door & got back at 7. *Bordering on love-making in the hut - said I should certainly take her off with me - hoped she could trust me. Yes, she had the greatest confidence in me, & our going together was actually agreed on - & we afterwards talked of it as a thing settled, depending only on our respective aunts, both of whom [are] in a precarious way.*

> *Our liaison is now established - it is to be named to nobody but her sister & aunt & my aunt, & that not till a week or ten days before our being off. We shall now go on swimmingly & our courtship will progress naturally - she already likes me - perhaps she scarce knows how [much], & we shall both be in love seriously enough before our journey.*

> *I should breakfast at Lightcliffe tomorrow & [would say I] could not resist calling as I returned, to ask if she had got cold - if she is out, I am to go to her at Cliff-hill. My aunt had hoped she would come on Monday, to which she readily consented - so that we shall probably see a good deal of each other. She looks happy & as if the remainder of the victory to be won would not cost me too much difficulty. Thought I, as I returned, 'Well, M- set me at liberty in May - in less than five months I am reprovided [for] & the object of my choice have [ie has] perhaps three thousand a year or near it, probably two-*

thirds at her own disposal.[85] *No bad pis aller*[86] *- even if I liked her less - a better take than Lady Gordon or perhaps Vere either. Well, now I will be steady & constant & make the poor girl as happy as I can, so that she shall have no reason to repent.*

On my return home, found on my desk [a] parcel: the letter-press (presse-papier) & note from Miss Walker - explaining about [her tenant] Collins & that she should hope to find me in my walk between 3 & 5.[87] [It] begins with 'I have real pleasure in sending the letter-press...'

We are in smooth waters now - she tells me more & more of her affairs - she feels at ease & happier with me than perhaps she could easily explain, & probably we shall both be impatient by & by to be off. I myself am surprised at my so rapid success & at the novelty of my situation. Perhaps after all, she will make me really happier than any of my former flames - at all rates we shall have money enough & I don't fancy she will either be close or stingy or cold to me. Had just written the above of today at 8¾. How little my aunt thinks what is going on! M- believes me safe at home & dreams not how she is losing all chance of me - she is right served [served right].[88]

Nobody working for me today (except Pickles & co at the weaving) but Dick getting on & spreading ashes.

Anne Lister's practised courtly flattery could also be extended to her old confidante.

Saturday 29 Off to Lightcliffe at 7 25/", there at 8 - waited some time before Mrs Priestley came down - sat ¾ hour at breakfast with Mr & Mrs P-. Then an hour's reading volume 7, Paley's works[89] till she had done her several jobs - then sat talking very confidentially & agreeably from about 10½ to 2. *Very good friends - told her I had lately*

---

[85] ie, not entailed (by the terms of her father's will).

[86] Last resort.

[87] SH:7/ML/612, received 28.9.1832 (re meeting 'at your little garden gate.)

[88] AL's code here elsewhere becomes a little haphazard in her excitement.

[89] William Paley (1743-1805) was her father; it was perhaps his *Evidence of Christianity*, 1794.

*heard it said she was a very fascinating person - all I said was kind &
friendly as ever & perhaps more flattering than usual… at which she seemed
not displeased. Quite as friendly, open & consulting as ever to Mr P-.* Mrs
P- asked me to dinner at 4 but I declined, saying I had already made
quite a visitation - said I had intended calling at Cliff-hill, but it was
too late – said [I] would call on the other Miss Walker instead.

At Lidgate at 2 5/", Miss W- had dined & would go with me to Cliff-
hill, if I could wait till 4 - sat talking till off at 4₃/₄ - & found Miss [ie
aunt] Walker at home, glad to see us & persuaded us to stay to tea[90] -
came away at 7. Sat 1/2 hour with Miss W- at Lidgate, & home in 1/2
hour at 8₁/₄.

*We now get on beautifully - I obscurely love-making & she all smiles - said
felt sure of my own happiness & I might be equally so of hers. 'Oh, she was
sure of hers', but had been thinking last night whether she could make me
happy & be a companion for me. She said how happy she now felt & looked
so, as we sat on the sofa…* [91]

*In moralizing a little on how much we had both to be thankful for, how happy
we should be etc - she said 'Yes, she had often looked at all her things & said
what was the use of having them with nobody to enjoy them with her?' She
said it all seemed now like a dream to her - I told her I had made up my mind
in May – the moment I was at liberty to do so*[92] *– so that it had been well
enough digested by me, however sudden it might seem to her - & that I gave
my happiness into her keeping in perfect security - said I had built the hut on
purpose for her – talked of our journey.*

She is to have [her friends] *Mr & Mrs Ainsworth in February – they
cannot come before – she wishes not to put them off &, all other things
suiting, would rather not go* [away] *till February. Said I would wait for her.*

*Talked of (& advised her) letting her house at Lidgate – to our steward
Washington - she would never want it again – as long as there was room for
us at Shibden –* [I] *laughed and said 'Let Cliff-hill' - but on her saying 'Cliff-*

---

[90] She would be delighted that her niece had such a respectable friend as Miss Lister
of Shibden Hall.

[91] Sofaof course had louche connotations

[92] May: AL, not mentioning either VH or M-, was being very economical with the
truth.

hill!' – [I] *thought it was too early in our day to mention, & said I was only joking. But I shall manage it all by & by – she is getting more & more attached to me, & I really do begin to be in love in good earnest. Her countenance lightens up, she looks happy & I begin to think her at times pretty. I begged her to take up her French & sketching again - & we already begin to feel at home together - & very much (however little she may understand it) like engaged lovers.*

Her servant came home with me with a lantern to Mytholm hill – where I sent him back, on meeting Cordingley & Rachel. My aunt has been miserable about my being out so late, & Marian set on me on my entering the room - that I must do so [ie stay out late] no more etc etc, in that sort of, to me, appearing dictatorial manner, that I as usual could not stand it, & it ending in Marian's crying & having a nervous fit.

However all got round again at last & I stayed up till 11 with my aunt *- telling her my real sentiments about Miss Walker & my expectations - that the chances were ten to one in favour of our travelling & ultimately settling together. My aunt not to appear to know anything about it, even to Miss* [aunt] *W- till I had mentioned it to the latter. My aunt* [said] *it had really come into her head as she sat in the drawing-room this* [yesterday] *afternoon - & seemed very well pleased at my choice & prospects. I said she had three thousand a year or very near it, as I had understood some time since from the Priestleys. She thought my father would be pleased if he knew, & so would both my uncles. Came upstairs at 11.*

Of course the relationship had to be kept very discreet: even Anne's aunt was told of Anne's 'expectations' only through allusion to foreign travel and to Ann Walker's fortune and income. However, her aunt's love for her unusually talented and affectionate niece was unqualified, and so she was prepared – surprising as it may seem - to view Anne's 'choice & prospects' in conventional dynastic terms, just as Anne did.

Anne preferred feminine women, who 'took up' French and sketching. On Ann Walker's part, it must have been flattering to have had built for you a moss house looking down over idyllic meadows and a stream. Already they were *'like engaged lovers'*. But in Anne Lister's planning about *which* house they would in future live in, a subject of such symbolic importance to her, she had been a little hasty. Ann Walker was happy to make personal adjustments, less willing to acquiesce when it entailed public changes.

Meanwhile, the Shibden household continued each Sunday to work its way systematically through the sermons of Reverend Samuel Knight, the late Vicar of Halifax.

> **Sunday 30** *Awake at five & from then to getting up lay thinking of Miss W-; at nine incurred the cross – I really am getting much more in love than I expected to be again – in fact, she likes me, it is evident - & I think we shall be very happy together.* Breakfast with my aunt.... Then read *prayers & sermon (11) Mr Knight in 55 minutes....*[93] *Stayed downstairs talking till 4 20/" - just gently named to Marian, when alone with her, that I really wished she would never again set at me as she did last night - & she began roaring again, saying we did not suit & she* <u>*would*</u> *go away etc etc. This always annoys me, & at last I am inclined to make it a rule never to mention Marian in any way to anyone.*

In the Shibden household, the scales were turning: Marian was becoming in thrall to her elder sister. Indeed, Anne's September ended with one tumultuous, action-packed week, when all her plans, carefully laid over the summer, bore fruit.

She had lived through the marriage of Mariana and seen her, a doctor's daughter, move to the Lawton estate; she was all too familiar with the family calculations that determined where the couple should live after the wedding. It was surely appropriate here for the daughter of a *nouveau riche* mercantile family to move into the home of ancient landed gentry, rather than vice versa.[94] And, after all, Shibden dated back to the early fifteenth century, while Cliff-hill was scarcely sixty years old. Also, Anne Lister refused to give Shibden up to Marian. Her desire for inherited gentry status was probably as powerful as her desire for love and a life-

---

[93] *Sermons... & Miscellaneous Works of the Rev Samuel Knight...*, Halifax, 1828, vol II; Sermon XI – 'I have sworn, and I will perform it, that I will keep thy righteous judgements'. Knight had earlier taught Anne

[94] For delicate courtship & pre-nuptial negotiations, see Amanda Vickery, *The Gentleman's Daughter: women's lives in Georgian England* (1998), pp 45-58; also Perkin, *Women & Marriage*, pp 51-3.

companion. And so the conversation necessarily turned upon each woman's expectations and prospects.

October

Monday 1 Waited to wish Marian a pleasant journey to Market Weighton per Highflier [coach] at 11 am – out again at 9$_{1/4}$ - along the walk by Lower brea & the new road to meet Miss W-, & met her near Hipperholme lane-ends at 9 50/". We rested in the hut, & she being not quite strong & well (obliged to go out of afternoon church yesterday in the middle of the service), advised her not going farther & walked home with her. *We sat from a little past ten to ten minutes to four – [a] sign she was not tired of my company… Said how kind my aunt would be to her, how pleased she was etc.*

Proposed her living with me at Shibden & letting Cliff-hill - she spoke of her great attachment to the latter – I advocated skilfully &, I think successfully, the advantages of Shibden – and said that less money needed be paid out [for domestic improvements] than she perhaps imagined. Explained that there would be more <u>éclat</u> & independence even for <u>her</u> at Shibden than at Cliff-hill - & that she had but a life interest in the one [ie Cliff-hill] & might [have] the same in the other [ie Shibden].[95]

Said I expected to have ultimately two thousand a year[96] *- she told me it was more than she expected from my manner of speaking before. I then asked if she thought she could be happy enough with me, to give up all thought of ever leaving me. This led her into explaining that she had said she would never marry - but that, as she had once felt an inclination not to keep to this, she could not yet so positively say she should never feel the same inclination again. She should not like to deceive me & begged not to answer just now. I said she was quite right – praised her judiciousness – that my esteem & admiration were only heightened by it – that no feelings of selfishness should make me even wish [for] my happiness rather than hers – that I would give her six months, till my next birthday… to make up her mind in, & [I] should only hope that, as we saw more of each other, my reasons for despair would not increase. She thought I had given her a long [time]. We then rallied each*

---

[95] life interest: AW owned the Cliff-hill half of the Crow-nest estate only for her lifetime; see *FF* pp 33-8.

[96] Ultimately: presumably on the death of her father and aunt, when AL would receive all Shibden's rents.

other… To all my thorough love speeches (of anxiety and impatience) hoping she would not think me foolish, she invariably replied, 'Indeed'…. On the plea of feeling her pulse, I took her hand & held it some time – to which she shewed no objection - in fact, we both probably felt more like lovers than friends. I said, if she felt a quarter the regard for me [as] I did for her, I should be satisfied – but if she ever felt half, I should be <u>more than happy</u> - she said that would come - in fact, I think it will.

Marginalia *Gave her (first thing I ever did give, save the key of the walk gate…[97]) one - the last but one I have - of the little gold gondola brooches I brought from Venice.*

I had said she had more heart & more of something like romance than her sister [Elizabeth] *- 'Yes' - she told me she always thought I had a tincture of romance about me. I praised her penetrat[ration]. It seems she had observed & felt my manner of sitting by her when she called with her uncle & aunt Atkinson – I said, that was done because I really could not help it, or I should have sat by Mrs Atkinson. She said she had thought of me every <u>day</u> at Wastwater… She had always an idea that her thirtieth year would be a very important one.*

She already feels towards me she scarce knows what, & is surely in the high-road to being in love. Yes, I think she will take me. I see I must be uncommonly & fastidiously delicate. I wanted to hint at the propriety of her leaving me for a minute or two on our getting to Lidgate – but she was too modest to seem to understand me at all. I see there is evidently coming on all the shyness usual in such cases [ie betrothed young women?] *Well, I shall like her all the better for it & am already fairly in love myself.*

Read her what M- said in her last [letter] *about Eugénie & said what I had written. Much confidential conversation - I had near been in Spain – might have settled with a woman of rank & fashion & two thousand a year (alluding to Lady Gordon) but could not make up my mind till I knew what chance I had elsewhere – fancy* [romantic imagination] *all powerful etc etc. Yet amid all, she never let slip her own income.*

We sat from soon after ten to ten minutes to four in the hut. Then saw her home – sat till she had had some gruel & biscuit & wine…. & left her at six & a half. Thought I, 'She is in for it, if ever a girl was - & so am I too.' Walked leisurely home by the new road – sat a little while in the hut & home

---

[97] Probably the gate at the top of walk leading into garden immediately in front the house.

at 6½... Sat up talking to my aunt.

For Anne Lister, Elizabeth Sutherland had opted for merely a conventional marriage. She hoped that Ann Walker would, unlike Mariana and Vere, hold steadfastly to genuine romantic feeling – as she herself did. During their six hours in the moss house, Anne was courtly and plausible, Ann Walker romantic though shy. They held hands like lovers. Certainly Anne, with firm notions of courtship proprieties and rituals, dropped hints about Eugénie and European travel.[98]

Thursday 4 At Lidgate in ½ hour at 10.... *She stated as [two] difficulties the not living at Cliff-hill & my intimacy with the William Priestleys – she would do as she liked about the former – [I said] it was herself, it was person, not place I cared for - & as soon as all was settled, my giving up the P-s was easy & natural.*

This said, she seemed reconciled & satisfied – I said I would listen to no difficulty, but the pre-engagement of her own heart - she declared it not engaged - & talked of letting the Ainsleys [Ainsworths] have Cliff-hill as if she had determined on being with me at Shibden...

I had my arm on the back of the sofa – she leaned on it – looked as if I might be affectionate, & it ended in her lying on my arm all the morning & my kissing her & she returning it with such a long continued passionate or nervous mumbling kiss – that we got on as far as we, by day-light, mere kissing, could - I thinking to myself, 'Well, this is rather more than I expected – of course she means to take [me]'. Yet on pressing the hardness of my case [ie situation] in having to wait six months, & begging for a less length of probation – she held out, saying her mind was quite unmade up - & I must not hope too much for fear of disappointment.

Yet she asked me to dine with her at five & stay all night – I promised the former. Very sorry could not do the latter while my father was unwell & my sister absent. Thought I, 'I see I shall get all I want of her person [body], if I stay all night'.

Back at five to dinner - she had put on an evening gown - & a sort of set-out

---

98 AL also gave her father his medicine

dinner for me[99] *– I talked much of the Highlands etc while the man*[servant] *was there. Afterwards drew near to each* [other] *& she sat on my knee, & I did not spare kissing & pressing, she returning it as in the morning. Yet still I was not to hope too much - she said I was infatuated – when the novelty was over I should not feel the same – and I might not find her a companion for me. I waived all this, fancying all her scruples were of this sort.*

On leaving the dining room, we sat most lovingly on the sofa - thought her aunt would not live six months – said she had a fancy for Eugénie. If we were not ready for her by January, we were to allow her something [ie wage] *& retain her.*

We were so affectionate – we let the lamp go out – long continued (mumbling moist) kissing, I prest her bosom - then finding no resistance & the lamp being out – let my hand wander lower down, gently getting to [her] *queer – still no resistance – so I whispered surely she could care for me some little?*[100] *'Yes'. Then gently whispered she would break my heart if she left me – she then said I should think her very cold (how the devil could I?) & it came out: how that her affections had been engaged to one of the best men – that they could not be transferred so soon - for he had only been dead just three months - & she got to crying. I begged a thousand pardons etc etc – declared it was only thro' ignorance that I had ever been so sanguine etc etc - & thinking a scene would then come beautifully from me, seemed in a paroxysm of stupid tho' deeply sighing grief & stifled tears - & declared myself hopeless* [ie without hope] *– said my conduct (or rather, my hoping) was madness... All this was very prettily done.*

I however promised to see her tomorrow & we parted in all the pathos due to the occasion. I said little as I returned to poor John [servant] *– musing on the curious scene of today. 'Cold', thought I! 'No sign of that – more likely, she will try what I can do for her before giving the answer, & I don't think I can do enough.' She had said that if she once made up her mind she thought herself as much as married to me for life. Well, I may try her, or rather let her try me - & go* [to] *what lengths the first night I sleep there. She certainly gulled me in that I never dreamt of her being the passionate little person I find her, spite of her calling herself 'cold'. Certainly I should never have*

---

[99] AW seemed to have had some kind of anorexia, which might explain her not eating.

[100] 'Queer" seems to mean female pudenda; see *Helena Whitebread, No Priest But Love: the journals of Anne Lister 1824-1826*, 1992, p55

ventured such lengths just yet without all the encouragement she gave me. I shall now turn sentimentally melancholy & put on all the air of romantic hopelessness. If I do this well, I may turn her to pity... I scarce know what to make of her. Is she maddish? I must mind what I say to her. <u>Be cautious</u>...

Hang it! This queer girl puzzles me. She told me this morning of the weakness in her back, for which she uses Mr Day's ointment - it was from making her walk too soon when an infant. I think a little spice of matrimony would do her good.

At Lidgate from 10 to 2½ then home... back in ½ hour at 5 to Lidgate to dinner – home in ½ hour at 10½... Note today from the H-x philosophical society to say there would be a meeting of subscribers tomorrow... Miss W- much troubled with anonymous letters – said she would get rid of all troubles of cousins or letters when with me.[101]

In the seduction, Anne Lister had encountered little or no resistance. Her diary recorded the scene in a fairly calculating way. But perhaps this was just the understandable cynicism of any impecunious, slightly caddish suitor towards a neighbouring heiress?

However, it had not gone unnoticed that almost every day Anne Lister walked briskly to and from Lidgate. Indeed, Ann Walker had received anonymous letters, presumably from a well-wisher, warning her of Anne Lister's predatory reputation. And Ann Walker's grief was tangible at the so recent death of a suitor.

Friday 5 *At Lidgate at 10½ ... Home at 6½ & dinner at 7.... We somehow got more at ease again.... I explained how sorry I was - would have been the last to have intruded on her feelings etc etc – under circumstances of such recent grief – but... we would leave things as they always were – so far that I would not let her give her answer now, but wait the six months as agreed... still thought her answer would be 'no'. I said my expectations were very moderate - I should be satisfied if she could always be to me as she was now... I had resolution enough - & durst brave all.*

We then got much as yesterday - but [for] her bad back & she very languid as she lay on the sofa on my arm, I might have done what I liked - she gave

---

[101] Probably the Atkinsons (importunate) or William Priestley. No such anonymous letter survives in SH:7/ML; nor apparently among the Crow-nest papers.

*me her mumbling kisses again - & I seemed empassioned but still said I had
'no hope'...*

*I got up to go before four, but she asked me to stay - & I loitered & said how
little resolution I had. She said Catherine Rawson would suit me better – I
said 'No', & afterwards explained that I could not sufficiently respect her
common-sense.*

*On (before) wishing her to have Doctor Belcombe's opinion, she said he
would only laugh – all [doctors] would say 'what was the matter with
her?' (Meaning, that she wanted [ie lacked] a good husband). I of course
denied it – but thought it near enough the truth. She thinks me over head-&-
ears [in love?] with her - she is mistaken - her mumbling kisses have cured
me of that.*

*She was talking of [George] Crabbe's poems – Catherine maintained they were
not fit to be read – Miss Walker was not so particular – not fit for young girls,
but very well for herself & Catherine.[102] 'Oh, ho', thought I, 'this is a new light
[ie discovery] to me - likely enough from your manner'. She casually said the
other day, she should now know better how to flirt than she used to do - it has
struck me more than once, she is a deep-ish [ie sly] hand. She took me up to
her room – I kissed her & she pushed herself so to me, I rather felt & might
have done it as much as I pleased. She is man-keen enough - if I stay all night,
it will be my own fault if I do not have all of her I can....*

*She let out today that there is some[one] who would now be glad of her &
take her into a very different rank of life from her present one.[103] (Some poor
Scotch baronet?) At all [ie any] rates, I may handle her as I like - if I choose
to venture it. How changed my mind... I care not for her - tho' her money
would suit.... Have she & Catherine been playing tricks? But the latter is in
the wane with her now. I am cured.*

*Said [to my aunt this evening] I thought the thing would go off – for it
seemed as if she could not give up Cliff-hill & I could [not] leave Shibden.
Said how I was cooled about the thing - yet still that I would wait the six
months for the answer - if it was 'No', I should not grieve much... Putting
all on Shibden made my aunt take [it] all right.*

---

102 Among the poems of George Crabbe (1754-1832) was, for instance, 'Sir Eustace
Grey', set in a madhouse in which the protagonist killed his wife's lover in a duel and
was wracked by guilt.

103 Not Fraser, not Ainsworth; perhaps a relative or acquaintance of the Sutherlands

Dr Belcombe and conventional medical opinion might well believe that the health of unmarried women of Ann Walker's age would indeed be improved with 'a good husband'. But Anne Lister, now that she perceived Ann Walker as 'man-keen' rather than virginally pure, shifted her attitude towards her.[104]

Meanwhile, a letter came from Eugénie Pierre's sister: Eugénie would be ready in January, if Anne Lister would engage her. Anne made enquiries about her.

> **Saturday 6** A little while with my aunt. *She thought me looking uncommonly well & in unusually good spirits (& so in fact I felt) on the occasion of my [decision] (as I told her last night) giving up Miss Walker. Laughed - I felt as pleased that it was over as I had done when it began - thought whatever is, is right.* Out at 11½ - sauntered down my walk... Charles & James H- thatching the hut with another cover of rushes....
>
> [Mrs William Priestley and I] *very good friends... Somehow speaking of her* [Ann], *Mrs P- said we were very thick – I had been every day - it was a very good thing for her* [Miss W-] *– I ought to influence her to patronize this or that....* 'Yes, we were very good friends - I had not been every day – not Tuesday or Wednesday - but we could not hold on quite at our present [rate] – I should not go there today'.

Mrs Priestley's house and Lidgate were only a few minutes apart; she knew Anne of old and was very observant. But perhaps she was not sufficiently canny; and Anne Lister's social status as a 'patron' could, after all, only benefit as shy and isolated a young woman as Ann Walker. More generally, the very respectability of 'female friendship' provided the perfect cover by which Anne Lister might, on the grounds of allaying her aunt's fears, stay the night at Lidgate.

> **Sunday 7** Looking again at last night's paper & the last Gardener's Magazine[105] – off to church with my father at 10 down the old bank... Off to Lightcliffe at 3 50/"... Staid till 10... My aunt waiting [up] for

---

[104] The sexual double standard is well known: an elite woman would be expected to be a virgin on marriage

[105] *Gardener's Magazine,* and *Register of Rural and Domestic Improvement, 1826-44.*

me – had been frightened but said she would say nothing – I must stay all night in future.

[Miss W-] very glad to see me – began again about wishing me to have 'no hope'… [I] thinking to myself, 'After much pretty talk, I care little about it, anyway….' It seems I can have her as my mistress & may amuse myself - she kissed me & lay on my arm as before, evidently excited …

To prove I had 'no hope', said I had told my aunt so - yet I kissed & pressed very tenderly & got my right hand up her petticoats to [her] queer, but not to the skin – could not get thro' her thick knitted drawers, for tho' she never once attempted to put my hand away, she held her thighs too tight together for me. I shall manage it the next time…

Quizzed her for thinking we might be as comfortable [apart], she at Cliff-hill & I at Shibden, as if we were together. In fact, I may certainly have my own way, she all the time telling of her coldness. She asked me to spend the whole day & stay the night on Tuesday - I said I would breakfast with her. I wonder what she will say when I have once fairly <u>done my best for her</u>…

How little she dreams of all this - she thinks me over head-&-ears, past recall – her mumbling kisses & anything but coldness have done [me?] a world of good…. <u>Very</u> fine, delightful, moonlight night…. John came for me tonight & went first to the Priestleys - they will talk us over & think something is in the wind - [however] Mrs P- said yesterday my going to her (Miss W-) so much was a good thing for her.

Yet Anne Lister did not want another mistress or merely another flirtation. She wanted what Vere had so recently acquired: a serious relationship, a life-companion; indeed, she wanted a wife. Mrs Priestley had a notion of this; and she was sufficiently perceptive to take note of servant John's late-night visit. Meanwhile, Anne Lister walked down into Halifax.

Monday 8 To Throp's – above 2 hours there giving him a tolerably large order for evergreens & shrubs & a few trees etc to be sent to Shibden by noon tomorrow week. [106] Passed the old church at $1\frac{1}{2}$ and up the old bank & at Lidgate in 40 minutes…

We had a good deal of talk – I said happiness was, in well-bred minds, more

---

[106] AL also paid her first visit to Halifax's new philosophical & natural history museum, vowing to donate to its collection.

mental than in others - if such was, or could be, her feelings & she could give up the thought of having children, perhaps she might be happy with me etc etc.... Talked of their being no chance of <u>my</u> marrying – but I saw she did not quite enter into this, in spite of all the hints it seemed safe to give. Kissing & pressing her as usual – she put the blind down - lucky – James had come in on trivial errands twice.

And Mrs Priestley came at four – I had jumped in time & was standing by the fire – but Ann looked red & I pale, & Mrs P- must see we were not particularly expecting or desiring company. She looked vexed, jealous & annoyed & asked (in bitter satire) if I had [been] where I was ever since she left me there. 'No', said I, 'I only ought to have been. My aunt had been quite in a host of miseries'. Mrs P- said, as if turning it all on this, 'Yes, she [your aunt] was quite vexed with me.' I laughed & said I really did not intend doing so [causing her anxiety] again. 'Yes', she replied angrily, 'you will do the same the very next time the temptation occurs'. 'Plain proof', thought I, 'of what you think, & that you smoke [ie suspect] a little'. I parried all with good humour – saying that I really must stay all night. She only staid a few minutes & went off in suppressed rage today....

Miss W- laughed & said <u>we</u> were well-matched – we soon got to kissing again on the sofa.... At last I got my right hand up her petticoats & after much fumbling got thro' the opening of her drawers & touched (first time) the hair & skin of [her] queer – she never offered the least resistance...

When dusk, she asked (I had said I was at no time likely to marry – how far she understood me I could not quite make out): 'If you never had any attachment, who taught you to kiss?' I laughed & said how nicely that was said – then answered that nature taught me. I could have replied, 'And who taught <u>you</u>?'...

Left Lidgate at 6 25/" ... Told my aunt how cross Mrs William Priestley looked, & that I really though Miss W- was veering about a little & might perhaps after all give up Cliff-hill.

Mrs Priestley no longer entertained illusions. However, any critical reservations by Anne's aunt, to whom the situation had been explained in terms of the two houses and estates, remained mightily blurred by her love for her unusual niece. Also, it was a world in which belief in respectable women's romantic friendships (for which the conventional precautions attached to heterosexual seduction were not needed) worked ironically to Anne's considerable advantage.[107]

> **Wednesday 10** Charles & James Haworth here today – mossed roof of hut, door & bench of ditto... [108] My aunt, tho' better these few days, has still spasms & says she feels weak.

As she grew more aware of its relative magnificence, Anne Lister responded to Ann Walker's wealth by loftily weaving into her own planned improvements some castellations and a new name: 'Shibden Castle'. At the same time, Ann Walker was already taking Anne Lister's advice not only about estate and family matters,[109] but also about her friends. And so when the conversation turned to the Ainsworths, for whom Ann wanted to obtain a local ecclesiastical living, Anne Lister could adroitly let slip vague aristocratic allusions to her own influence.

> **Thursday 11** Off to Lidgate at 7 10/" & there is 35 minutes (just before it began to drizzle and rain) along my walk. *Miss W- came down in two or three minutes – above an hour at breakfast... Got on very well - kissing as usual –* dinner at 2 in about 1/2 hour – did not take [eat] much - *afterwards love-making & kissing, she lying on my arm.*

> *Told her, as we got to talking more & more as if we should be together, that I thought of... castellating the new part[110] & the lodge (from the Godley road), changing the name to Shibden castle... that as soon as we had been settled together, I would settle Shibden [on] her for life.*

> *We talked of the Ainsworths coming to Cliff-hill - & getting Lightcliffe chapel* [ie living] *for him – she might be able to get the archbishop's interest*

---

[107] In 1819 a case against two Edinburgh women was found in their favour, as the 'crime here alleged has no existence'.

[108] AL, 10.10.1832, removed a good-sized holly from the front of the hut to fill up part of the old line of walk in Lower Brook Ing wood, ie she had shifted the walk near the moss house.

[109] Eg, SH:7/ML/614/1; & responding to begging letters from an Atkinson cousin.

[110] Probably the new walls along Shibden, built c1828 when a 30-foot cutting & embankment by Godley improved the turnpike road

[ie influence] *with our* [Halifax] *vicar - I feared that might be refused, but I could perhaps apply to the vicar thro' the next best channel (meaning, but not saying so, Lord Wharncliffe).*[111]

As it became dusk we crept closer & I, without any resistance, got (for the first time) right middle finger up her queer... She whispered that she loved me – then afterwards said her mind was quite unmade up & bade me not be sanguine.

The name of Cliff-hill escaped [from] *me & she burst into tears... How can I tell what to make of her? She had casually said Catharine Rawson had often said she should like to live with her - they had long ago talked of it - but now, & of late, she had thought it would not answer & was getting* [going] *off* [it]. *Thought* [I], *'then my surmise was probably true – when I fancied that Catherine's classics might have taught her the trick of debauching Miss W-'.*[112] *Yes, Miss W- has been taught by someone... And I said to myself as I walked along – 'Damn her, she is an old hand & has nor shame nor anything - she certainly takes all very much like one of the initiated.'* Home in 1/2 hour or 25 minutes at 6 50/" – drizzling rain.

At this point, electoral politics surfaced again.[113] Anne read about 'the late public breakfast & dinner given by the Whigs to their candidates Messrs Wood & Rawdon Briggs'; and she wrote to her southern friends about how 'we shall want the Duke of Wellington by & by', as 'things seem going on very queerly'.

Propertied women might be excluded from the parliamentary franchise, but they were still able to vote in smaller elections: one such local contest gave Anne Lister yet further insight into the complexities of Ann Walker's family property – on this occasion, the

---

[111] Lord Wharncliffe (1776-1845), the Yorkshire Tory peer, was father of James Stuart Wortley; AL's influence, presumably through Lady Stuart, was fairly negligible: however, it illuminates ecclesiastical politics, later depicted by Trollope

[112] This offers a clear statement about how, in AL's world, classical literature could signify secret sexual knowledge, with connections to latinate, Mediterrean travel & culture.

[113] Parliament was prorogued (ie discontinued) on Tuesday 16

Edwards family (Ann's uncle being, along with William Priestley, a trustee of her father's will).

Monday 15 *Washing & mending my stays till eight... had Cordingley to take trimming off <u>old</u> French silk petticoat.* Breakfast with my aunt at $10_1/2$ - Miss Walker came in 5 or 6 minutes – off with her at 11 [to Halifax] – shopped – sat in the carriage... Mr Edwards came to the carriage door to ask me to give my vote (from the Northgate property) [114] in favour of – I forget whom – against the radical candidate, Ramsden, for the [Halifax] constableship – the town in a bustle – voting at the Waterhouse Arms – the poll to close at 5pm. I had [not] heard, nor knew, anything about it; Mr E- had just voted in right of his executorship to the late-but-one Mr Walker of Crow-nest – odd enough to say this before his daughter sitting by me (who afterwards observed that she was now the 2nd in succession to that property). [115]

Went to Throp's... then called at a shop or 2, & at Lidgate at $5_1/4$ - dinner at 6 – very cozy evening. Miss W- read prayers [to her servants] we went upstairs at $10_1/4$ - fine day. *I undressed in half-hour & then went to her room – had her on my knee a few minutes & then got into bed, she making no objection - & staid with her till twelve & three-quarters - grubbling gently... She seemed so tender & able to bear so little (I think she was more <u>in tact</u> & innocent & [a] virgin than I had latterly surmised) that I contented myself with handling her gently & love-making. She feared she should never be able to satisfy me... She whispered to me in bed how gentle & kind I was to her, & faintly said she loved me, 'or else how can you think', said she, 'that I should let you do as you do?' In fact, tho' I never allow that I have 'hope', surely I ought not to despair – she surely cannot go on as she does, meaning to say 'no'.*

Tuesday 16 Miss W- not well – lay on the sofa all the day & I sat by her *very affectionately – gave her her gruel... nursed her very tenderly - the more so as she was suffering from having had me last night...[She] never thought I should have made her suffer so much – would never let me do so again. I took all this very well... and we talked as if there was no chance of*

[114] Elegant Northgate House in Halifax was part of the Shibden estate.

[115] The extensive Crow-nest estate included properties in Halifax; presumably AW's comment refers to her inheriting the Crow-nest half of the estate, if her sister Elizabeth Sutherland died.

her eventually refusing me... We settled to go to York on Monday... & have Dr Belcombe come to us.

Walked very fast and at home in less than 25 minutes at 6 50/" – dinner at 7 5/" – sat up talking to my aunt – *told her I really began to think Miss W- would give up Cliff-hill & come to me.*

Wednesday 17 Off at 8 40/" (along the walk) to Lidgate... She settled to have a sort of wing [of the house] glazed to form a green-house... *Very good friends... consulted me about her concerns – brought out her rent-roll... She told me yesterday, she had two* [thousand] *five hundred a year - & I should guess about one thousand at her own disposal...*

Home at 1½ - found Throp had sent the plants – took John & went down to the hut at 2 – had Pickles & Dick from then till dark – the former planting...

Staid talking with my aunt – *about Miss W-, said the more I saw of her, the more I felt satisfied with her etc etc.*

Anne Lister at last knew Ann Walker's financial situation: she was indeed wealthy.[116]

Thursday 18 At Lidgate to breakfast at 8 10/".... Hepworth (the joiner) came before we had done breakfast about the frame-work for the green-house to be made... *She said she should like the green-house, as it was the first thing we had a common interest in – talked of Shibden & Cliff-hill - & exactly as if all was settled – she was now convinced I loved her...*

At the weaving at 2 20/"... near the dam-stones at Mytholm...[117] John planting out Spanish chestnuts, roses, junipers, yews, violets etc in the walk.

Yet Anne Lister remained unhappy about Ann Walker's wanting her relationship with Anne to be almost more that of a mistress

---

[116] 'Wealth' was relative; AW was 'wealthy' for the Halifax area – but not, of course, by the standards of parts of England with vast estates. Although AL makes no comment about AW's remark about the Crow-nest estate, its significance will have been noted.

[117] Presumably near Tilly Holm.

rather than a wife: '*I know she would like to keep me on, so as to have the benefit of my intimacy without any real joint concern.*'

> **Saturday 20** Had Charles & John Booth with 2 poles (stangs) tied to an arm-chair & at 12₁/2 in an hour they carried my aunt to the bottom of my walk... to see the new line of cut for the brook – 'nothing could answer better' – my aunt much pleased & not at all tired... Off to Lidgate at 2₁/2...

Anne Lister wrote carefully to Mariana Lawton about how 'my neighbour Miss Walker' would consult her brother, Dr Belcombe. But Mariana was not 'to name it'.

> **Sunday 21** *Lay thinking & wavering about Miss W-... determined to amuse myself* <u>en libertin</u> *- & care no more about her.... Then preparing for my journey... sewing & busy over one thing or other...*Off at 6₁/4 to Lidgate – there in 25 minutes – tea at 9 in 20 minutes, read sermon... & prayers – came upstairs at 10... *I grubbling gently, she nothing loth.*[118]

On Monday, they set off in Ann Walker's carriage to York, where Dr Belcombe visited them.

> **Tuesday 23** Dr B- came at 8₁/2 - he staid near 1/2 hour with her & then as long with me in my dressing room – *nothing the matter with her but nervousness - if all her fortune could fly away & she had to work for her living, she would be well. A case of nervousnesss & hysteria* [119] *– no organic disease - thought I should be sadly pothered with her abroad unless I had the upper hand - & ought not to pet her too much - but going abroad would do her good.*

Dr Belcombe knew Anne Lister of old, so probably guessed the relationship between the two women. They then set off home.

> **Thursday 25** At Tadcaster in an hour... and in 3₁/2 hours (at 9 40/") alighted at Lidgate, Miss W- much less tired & having borne the journey much better than I expected - *I had felt her queer a little on leaving Leeds, it being dark - we talked quite as if all was settled - said I could not now spend more than a thousand pounds a year – talked of*

[118] 'Grubble' means grope, but perhaps also included caress or fondle; it apparently became obsolete by 1719.

[119] A possible link to a disturbance of the uterus.

alterations at Shibden - to [buy] *bed, one out of our joint income, supposing us to spend in travelling only two thousand a year. Talked of what plate we had, & seemed quite agreed - tho' without any decided 'yes' on her part.*

Anne Lister felt a confidence in the relationship - even without Ann Walker's long-awaited 'yes'. They enjoyed the detailed domestic auditing of what china they jointly possessed and planned to purchase a bed. It was surely virtually settled. Yet Anne's romantic desires were to be disrupted by news from an unexpected quarter.

FORMS

OF

PRAYER,

FOR THE USE OF

CHRISTIAN FAMILIES,

BY THE

REV. SAMUEL KNIGHT, A. M.

Late Vicar of Halifax.

NINETEENTH EDITION.

TO WHICH IS ADDED

A SECOND SERIES,

BY THE

REV. JAMES KNIGHT, A. M.

PERPETUAL CURATE OF ST. PAUL'S CHURCH,
SHEFFIELD.

THIRD EDITION.

HALIFAX:

PRINTED AND SOLD BY N. WHITLEY:

LONGMAN, REES, ORME, BROWN, AND GREEN; G. B
WHITTAKER; HURST, CHANCE, AND CO.; HAMILTON
AND ADAMS; BALDWIN AND CRADOCK; AND
J. RICHARDSON, LONDON.

MDCCCXXIX.

Forms of Prayer for the Use of Christian Families,
Rev Samuel Knight, Whitley, Halifax, 1829

6. THE IMPORTUNATE AINSWORTH

26 October - 1 December

October

Friday 26 *Grubbling till late & gave her, as she owned, pleasure…*[120] *[but] that I had no business to think her fairly my own till we had been really & properly together - & this led to doubts & fears on my part - & she talked of not deciding till the third of April* [ie AL's birthday]. Breakfast at 11 – sat talking till after 2 – then walked slowly along the village [ie Lightcliffe] to Cliff-hill - 1ˢᵗ went to see the carriage & then made our call.

The letter with black-edged paper & black seal from Miss Bentley [Ainsworth's sister-in-law], Manchester, being given to Miss W-junior to read – it fell from her hand on seeing that it was to announce the death of her friend Mrs Ainsworth, in consequence of being thrown out of an open carriage…

Immediately proposed our returning – walked home with Miss W-, & instead of going to Shibden as I had intended, wrote & sent at 5 little note to my aunt, stating the case & begging her not to expect me today…

Miss W- & I had had much talk (this morning) about bringing the Ainsworths here[121] *- & about money matters etc – seem to have persuaded* [her] *to let Lidgate… How all these Ainsworth plans are changed & over! Miss W- seemed much affected… It instantly struck me – she would in due time succeed her friend & be*[come] *Mrs Ainsworth. However, she had just said, 'Well, now there is no obstacle to our getting off in January'*. Wrote the journal of yesterday & so far of today till prayers at 10.

Anne was more prophetic about the impact of the Reverend Ainsworth's bereavement than she realised.

Sunday 28 Miss W- & I read aloud the Psalm & chapters… *Talked of*

---

[120] 'Grubble' means grope, but perhaps also included caress or fondle; it apparently became obsolete by 1719

[121] Presumably, the Lightcliffe living for Ainsworth.

*the Ainsworths – she meant to have asked Mrs A- on the propriety of
accepting me – whether it would be doing right to her property in leaving
Cliff-hill etc. It seems probably Mrs A- would have decided her on this point
of right & wrong - & that all scruples have been on this score. Of course, I
argued that the welfare of her family & property would be by no means
sacrificed by her being [at Shibden] with me. Perhaps I argued successfully -
& her scruples are really giving way?*

Anne's solicitous care of Ann Walker's health in York had
impressed Mrs Priestley.

Monday 29 Out with Miss W- at 11$_1$/$_2$ - walked with her by Crow-
nest... the ground before the house on this side very rough, & all
looking forlorn. Then to Cliff-hill – 10 minutes there & walked back
from there with Mrs William Priestley... *We were very good friends – I
told her Doctor B-thought Miss W- ought to get off & leave all pother
behind. Mrs P- thought she would take it with her. I said I would go over
again with her to York & do anything I could...*

Back at Lidgate at 4 – *she shewed me the joint property rentall – which was
last half-year – sixteen hundred & forty nine pounds... [with] none of the
joint property being entailed & the navigation stock [ie canal shares] being at
her own disposal.*[122]

Anne Lister, always so astute about money, was pleased to
discover how much of Ann Walker's inherited fortune was 'at her
own disposal' and so could be spent as she wished. Indeed, with the
relationship seemingly developing well, Anne was apparently even
prepared to live at Lidgate.[123]

Wednesday 31 *Grubbled last night but quiet this morning – talking things
over. Added to former difficulties, she thought she might not be fit for the
society I should wish – argued her out of this - & at last got her to shorten
the time of waiting for her final answer from three April to one January. She
seemed satisfied this would be better – should be settled before we set off [at]
the end of January for the continent - she seems less & less likely to say 'no' –*

---

[122] Under AW's father's will, on the death of their brother, AW and her sister
Elizabeth became co-heiresses; see *FF* p. 33-7.

[123] Why had AL changed her mind about this? Was it the size of AW's unentailed
property? Or was it just a temporary tactic?

in fact we talk & act as if 'yes' was all but said. Breakfast at 10...

We are to be off the end of January, back next autumn & go for a month to Scotland & then return - & plant at Shibden & do our business at home [ie Lidgate], *keeping up our travelling establishment, & being off again as soon as we could. Thought we could live in sufficiently good style at Lidgate for a thousand a year.*

Thursday 1 Out at 12 40/" – called and sat 20 minutes with Mrs W. Priestley at Lightcliffe *who talked almost exclusively to Miss W-.*[124] From Mrs W. P-, went to Cliff-hill & home at 2 5/". Miss W- had dined immediately – [I] just sat down and took a mouthful with her, meaning to be off to Shibden. *But she begged me to stay till she had read her letter from Mr Ainsworth, & this occasioned us such dolefuls* [ie grief] *that I offered to stay till tomorrow & wrote to this effect to my aunt...*

Mr Ainsworth hopes Miss W- will not forsake him as a friend – and begs her to write to him, without mentioning to Miss Bentley (his sister-in-law) his having written to Miss W-. 'Oh ho', thought I, 'all this is very clear' – and I candidly told her what I thought.... This led to my saying that she must now decide between Mr A- and me... and it ended in her resolving to give me her final answer on Monday – to write to Mr A- on that day – and shew me her letter.

A little cold meat brought in for me at 6¼ - tea at 6¾ - *sat by her on the sofa – both of us perpetually with silent tears trickling down our cheeks - she quite undecided - fearing she should not be so happy with him as she might have been - never knew till now how much she was attached to me - should make comparisons, too, in poor Mr Fraser's favour - and torturing herself with all the miseries of not knowing what to do. She said how beautifully I behaved... felt repugnance to forming any connection with the other sex. It was only on the twenty-eight of July last that Mr Fraser died - she was twenty-nine on the twentieth of May. We were doleful & tearful as ever & went upstairs to bed at 9 35/"*[125] *– very fine day - F59₁/₂⁰ at 9¾.*[126] *She says she is quite undecided - yet promises me a lock of queer's hair in the*

---

[124] This subtle social cutting of AL signified criticism of her behaviour, without it being expressed in words.

[125] Interesting that this is not written in code? Possibly a romantic friendship reference?

[126] Has AL brought her own thermometer? Or does AW have one too?

morning – and I am to cut it myself if I like!

Orphaned when she was nineteen, her only brother dying when she was twenty-six, and Mr Fraser just shortly after her twenty-ninth birthday, for Ann Walker death and sex swirled in a cauldron of guilt and grief. An unprotected heiress living alone, she was understandably wary about whom she could *really* trust.

Anne Lister, on the other hand, just wanted to make a prudent match and settle down for the remainder of her life. But now she found herself living out some extreme tensions. In particular, Ann Walker's tantalising behaviour, abnegating sexual responsibility, was very hard for Anne – who was understandably almost beside herself amid the contradictions.

They were out in a world without a script. In their despair, the two women fell into female and male roles: Ann Walker offering small domestic services, and Anne holding herself with dignity - and returning home to transact estate business.

Friday 2 *We fretted ourselves to sleep last might - she lay on me as usual to warm her stomach & then lay in my arms – but I was perfectly quiet & never touched her queer – the tears silently trickling from my cheeks down hers. Somehow I was shockingly <u>attendri</u> [softened] - tho' perpetually saying to myself 'Well, I care not how she decides…'.*

On awaking found myself as tearful as ever - just before getting up, I got scissars [scissors] – took up her night-chemise & attempted to cut the lock, but kissed her queer - gave her the scissars - said she must cut it for me herself - & threw myself into the great chair. She soon gave me the <u>golden</u> lock - threw herself on the chair by me. We wept (& kissed) – I thanked her & she left me.

F51₁/2º at 8₁/2 am & damp drizzling morning – packed my travelling bag - downstairs & breakfast at 10. Both of us <u>attendries</u> & the tears starting perpetually - I said my mind was made up for the worst – she said 'Well, but she had not given her answer yet'….

She would (& did) mend my gloves – begged me to promise to let her have a night-chemise for a pattern – but she saw I declined promising. She hoped she should do many more things for me – never knew till now how much she was attached to me. I made no reply… she hung upon me & cried & sobbed aloud at parting… 'Well', said I to myself as I walked off, 'a pretty scene we have had, but surely I care not much & shall take my time of suspense very quietly - & be easily reconciled either way'.

Home in less than 1/2 hour – it rained all the way, & latterly pretty smartly - sat talking to my aunt *but nothing about Miss W-.* Mr Jeremiah Rawson came at 12 40/" & staid 40 minutes, not meaning, he said, to have gone away without bargaining [about a coal lease]... Mr J. R- said he thought I should have been more reasonable – [I] said if he knew me at all, he would know that I should not swerve from what I said.

Jeremiah Rawson, another of Ann Walker's distant cousins, did indeed find Anne an extremely hard bargainer.

Meanwhile, Anne Lister now grew increasingly impatient with Ann Walker's refusal to take a tough line on Ainsworth's importuning letters, and with her nervous wavering about deciding 'yes' or 'no'.[127]

Then Anne received a revelatory note from Ann Walker - which taught her a lot more about Ann's recent emotional history. However, Anne was exceedingly displeased to discover that her destiny was apparently to be arbitarily determined merely by *'a slip of paper put in a purse'.*

Monday 5 Breakfast with my father at 8_{3/4} - shewed him the coal plan... At 11 Miss Walker's servant brought a basket for my aunt, and another to me, of grapes etc, *and* [a purse containing] *the note that ought to have said 'yes' or 'no' - I opened it in agitation, little expecting to find it a mere evasion - and all between us as undecided as ever...*[128]

Here is the copy of her memorable note: 'I send the promised note for your perusal & correction. I have endeavoured to express myself in the most gentle & delicate manner possible & rather to imply than say what I really mean. It is a most difficult note to write – and, had it been possible, I would rather have been silent for the present - until grief had become more subdued... I find it impossible to make up my own mind. For the last twelve months I have lived under circumstances of no common moment, and with my health impaired & with vivid regrets of the past, I feel that I have not the power

---

[127] SH:7/ML/619/1, 3.11.1832

[128] AL's diary entries here have been reordered; she wrote her comments and actions on AW's note, before transcribing the note itself. This I have reversed.

fairly to exercise my own judgement. My heart would not allow me to listen to any proposal of marriage, and this is in effect the same.[129] *I would simply go on & leave the event to God.*

And on these grounds, I once thought of asking if you would act upon your original intention, and consent for us to travel together for a few months. Again I feel this unfair to you. I promised an answer - and I am at your mercy. I have written the words ['yes' and 'no'] on a slip of paper & put them in the purse. I have implicit confidence in your judgement, & if you still think it better to decide today, the paper you draw out first must be the word [that decides] – or, if you prefer, let your good aunt draw. And then we neither of us decide - you may think this an evasive termination of my promise. Forgive me, for it is really all I can say. Having heard you say that in one case [ie if 'no'], I must give you up as a friend, I find myself as incapable of consenting to this, as I am for deciding under my present feelings what is to be my future course of life. Whatever may be the event, I shall always remain your faithful & affectionate A.W.'

Off to Lidgate at 11 10/" – rained all the way... *She was nervous when we met - but I looked calm & we soon got on tolerably - we kissed and she was affectionate as usual, as far as I would let her.....*

I returned the purse with the 'yes' at one end and the 'no' at the other, just as she had sent it – saying I could not leave to the decision of chance what ought only to be decided by her own heart. She felt the force of this remark - we both got attendries - and she begged me to give her a little more time... Promised her more time – for which she thanked me - and said I would stay then till after my rent-day on the second of January - begging however that she would not require longer than the first of January for her decision – which she promised. I explained that she really was wrong in putting the thing [ie paper in purse] as she had done - that a proud & honorable spirit could never brook such a strange trusting to chance...

I told her I had not been prepared for her note of this morning – either by... her last words to me on Friday... or by the lock of hair she had given. She said, 'Well, she had thought of this – she would not have given it [the lock] to anyone else!' 'And who', said I, 'could have asked it?'... There had been too many endearments and too great a tie between us, for me to go back to what I had been. Thus I have tacitly put an end to our travelling together so long as she is undecided... Better an end of it at once - her friendship would

---

[129] Possibly AL's plan is effectively a marriage proposal?

be an useless pother – and Steph's prudence, not to recommend too hastily the going abroad, was, he said, better for me.

But she said she could not now stay at home to be pothered with Mr A-'s letters & be without protection [ie of Anne] – she would gladly enough travel with me now. But why [should I] run the risk of spending my time and money for nothing? I shall be better without her - I can take Eugénie & go and live in a cottage near Grenoble - and study and improve myself and save my money...

On leaving her, I repeated myself: 'Come, nerve yourself up & never mind' - & on getting home said, 'Well, it is an arrow [ie sign] & perhaps a lucky escape. Thank God for all his mercies'...Wrote all but the first six lines of today – much the better for it – my mind more composed.

The palaver of the purse revealed a fundamental clash. Ann Walker, an orphaned heiress given to procrastination, preferred to leave her future to chance and to fate. In stark contrast, resolute and decisive Anne Lister, an equally observant Anglican, insisted that a 'proud and honorable' person should determine her *own* fate. Yet Ann continued to vacillate. Anne Lister even had to dictate Ann's discouraging letter back to the importuning Ainsworth.

Wednesday 7 *Miss W- nervous – in tears perpetually – I told her my plan of introducing her in York, where she might be very comfortable... Then spoke of Mr Ainsley [Ainsworth] – she was very nervous. At last, from little to more, it came out – that if she married him, it would be from duty – I pressed for explanation & discovered that she felt bound to him by some indiscretion – he had taught her to kiss, but they had never gone so far as she & I had done... On Mr A-'s account, my indignation rose against the parson - I reasoned her out of all feeling of duty or obligation towards a man who had taken such base advantage.*

She said there was now no other obstacle between us - & she should be happier with me... I asked her if she was sure of this. 'Yes, quite [sure]'. 'Well, then', [said] I, 'consider half-an-hour & decide'. In half the time she asked if I would take her & gave me her word & 'Yes' & hoped I should find her faithful & constant to me. Thus, in a moment that I thought not of, was I accepted & the matter settled. I kissed her.[130]

---

[130] In her excitement, AL's handwriting grew larger.

Anne Lister planned to order a ring from York to mark the seriousness of the settlement; but Ann Walker wrote, 'I cannot take it, my love, till I have fewer torments of conscience than I endure at present.'[131] Then Ann Walker received a six-page letter from Mr Ainsworth detailing his wife's last days and stressing her philanthropy; in a part marked private, he reminded Ann that *he* had been a friend to her in *her* affliction (presumably on the death of Mr Fraser), begging her to act as one to him now. Again, it was Anne Lister who firmly got Ann Walker to write back discouragingly. However, she was somehow able to turn Ainsworth's advances to her *own* purposes - with witty Mrs Priestley.

> **Saturday 10** At Lightcliffe at the William Priestleys at 8 55/"... For an hour while Mrs P- did her household business, reading the last... Blackwood's [Magazine] – favourable review of Gilpin's Practical hints upon land-scape gardening with some remarks on domestic architecture...[132] Then sat talking to Mrs W. P- till 1, chit-chat – *her praises of Mr Ainsworth – very evident how sure she makes [ie she was] of the match between him & Miss W-; & without either of us being too plain-spoken, we laughed & gave him for it till the tenth of this month next year – saying 'Pray remember the tenth of November' - &, if it prospers, Mrs P- to write & tell me. She said Mrs Ainsworth was very plain & much marked with small-pox & filled up the pittings with rouge – fifteen or 20 years older than her husband – who married her for money.*

Ainsworth's packages continued to plague Ann Walker, exacerbating her torments of conscience. [133]

> **Tuesday 13** Note from Miss W- (& Loudon's Encyclopedia of Gardening, & 2 volumes of Plutach's Lives)... Went down to my aunt for a few minutes to shew the fine pine[apple] Miss W- had sent her, & off to Lidgate at 2... *I seemed to have ceased to think of (or wish for) her*

[131] SH:7/ML/625, 9.11.1832.

[132] Rev William Gilpin (1724-1804), who had travelled across Britain in search of the picturesque, helped form attitudes towards gardens a generation earlier.

[133] Eg SH:7/ML/627/1 & 628/1, 12 & 13.11.1832.

as the future companion of my life... Made up the parcel [returned, unopened] *for Mr A-.*

Meanwhile, Anne was busy with 'stubbing' (ie cutting hedges down close to the root and uprooting); and Samuel Washington organised the draining of the old boggy Red Beck meander.

> **Friday 16** Some time with Pickles who begun the job I let him yesterday, filling up the old line of the brook. At Lidgate at 10₁/₂... *We had talked quite as if her going with me abroad was fixed –* [but] *she said she did not like going – felt as if she should never return & never durst let me leave her a moment in a foreign country. I parried all her arguments & she, seeming to submit, began to talk of arrangements... I see the best way is to speak as one having authority.*

Certainly, Ann Walker was scarcely the intrepid traveller Anne Lister dreamt of.

> **Sunday 18** Thinking how to plant up my walk with more hollies & thorns & yew & hazels .... *Thought very little of Miss W-, she has neither head nor heart for me – I shall be better without her, & yet I hesitate & know not how it will end.*

Other difficulties appeared too. First, Marian continued the spiky inheritance quarrel; she said she would leave Shibden after their father's death, and '*I observed that, after her once leaving here, she might see very little of me - she thought that probable & that she might see more of me abroad than in England.*'[134]

Next, with the general election looming, Lady Stuart wrote to ask for Anne Lister's 'interest for Mr Wortley' in Halifax. But Anne preferred her political influence to remain at arm's-length; her élite women friends, and their aspiring nephews, must *not* see her Shibden shabbiness.

> **Wednesday 21.** Kind letter tonight [from Lady Stuart]... [But I am] *pothered by Mr James Wortley's thanks for my good wishes - & [he] hopes to make my acquaintance. I shall say I am going to York, or be out of the way by some means or other – I am only afraid he will call.*

---

[134] AL, 19.11.1832

Exerting her 'authority', Anne Lister twice told Ann Walker that if she married, she would discover Anne had been as a meteor in her life: briefly and brilliantly dazzling, then disappearing like a dream.[135]

Friday 23 At Lidgate at 10$_1$/$_2$... *Miss W- doubting as usual whether she had done right in telling me about Mr Ainsworth - & saying she ought to have waited before pledging herself to me, could not go abroad... Parried her arguments, yet reminded her that I had said before 'I shall pass away like a meteor & leave no trace behind'... I am getting tired of her moody melancholy pother - & shall give her back her purse & 'Yes', & be off.*

Gardening offered tranquillity in a world of turmoil. Anne still liked to read up-to-the-minute gardening books which she ordered from Whitley's – along with a gift for Ann Walker.

Saturday 24 Out with Pickles & his son John stubbing & getting up thorns between Calf-croft & round Ing, & then between the 2 brook Ings,[136] &... planting... a bush of wild rose... near the hut...

Marginalia: Got today from Whitley's... (ordered some time since) Practical hints upon Landscape Gardening [with some remarks on domestic architecture, as connected with scenery], by William S. Gilpin... 1832, ...& a form of family prayers to be given to Miss W-.[137]

Anne now became quite angry about Ann and Ainsworth. The marriage she had so long sought was in danger of degenerating into just 'a friendship & corresponding'.

Sunday 25 Read aloud to my aunt, my father & sister & Hemingway [servant], the morning prayers & sermon (19) Mr Knight. At 1$_1$/$_4$ off along my walk to Lidgate... *She was low & looked disconsolate – had received the ring in memory of Mrs Ainsworth & that had put her into the dolefuls. Much talk of Mr A-; she will have him after all – I spoke with*

---

[135] AL, 19.11.1832

[136] These hedges were in immediate view just below the house; AL undoubtedly aimed to change this slope from an agricultural landscape to a landscape of leisure.

[137] The book titles are repeated in text and marginalia. AL had read *all* of Gilpin by Monday

indignation as usual, & she of duty... Then grubbled her, she making no sort of objection... In spite of all her declarations to the contrary, I begin to suspect he [Ainsworth] *really has deflowered & enjoyed her...*

She must have [had] *some man or other – I can never satisfy her – Steph was right enough about <u>hysteria</u>. 'Hang it, she has no shame... She is my mistress* [just] *for the time'.... I see she is for keeping up a friendship & corresponding. I told her not to call on me ever on my return, if she was Mrs Ainsworth – she would then be no longer the same person as now - & I, being the older resident in the neighbourhood, I should consider it my place to call on her, the option of visiting lying with me. She said she had once thought of his taking her name - I said I should* [still] *not consider him society for me - & under such circumstances, what friendship could be carried on between her & me?*

Then, as if things could not get worse, on Anne's way home 'an impertinent fellow with a great stick in his hand' lunged at her; 'God damn you', she retorted, pushing him away. And additionally, the Rawsons continued to haggle with her over coal.

Monday 26 Mr Jeremiah Rawson came at $9_1/2$ for about $1/2$ hour – he asked if I would take £200 per acre – said I had had £230 bid...

Read from page 151 to 228 (end) of Gilpin's on <u>Landscape Gardening</u>. Then wrote 3 pages to Dr Belcombe, Minster Yard, York, over which I could not help laughing... really think his medicines have done [Ann] good... 'The mind is worse than the body - &, in this respect, I confess, I find a nervous young lady much more difficult to manage than I expected'.

At this time, certain male homosexual acts were punishable by hanging; the law was silent about women - and this silence troubled Ann Walker. Harriet Parkhill, a more suspicious female companion, had arrived at Lidgate; she disapproved of the relationship with Anne Lister – and might stir up gossip.

Tuesday 27 At Lidgate in $1/2$ hour... *Appealed to her reason & put my arguments on the basis of religion – she seemed rather inclined towards me at last... She had doubted whether it was right to engage herself to me, if this sort of thing was so bad between two men, it must be so. I answered this in my usual way: it was my natural & undeviating feeling etc etc. 'But', said I,* *'the moral responsibility is already incurred'*[138] - *she seemed better satisfied... She would not let Miss Parkhill go to Pye-nest... by herself for fear evidently of her gossiping about us.* Returned by my walk.

Thursday 29 Down the old bank [to Halifax]... took the form of prayers I have got for Miss W- to Whitley's, ordering it to be bound in crimson morocco [leather], with purple watered silk fly-leaves & richly guilt [gilt].

Friday 30 Sat by Miss W-'s bedside till 2 when she got up – *she had been fretting all yesterday... As to its being wrong – this objection she seems to have almost got over.*

Ann Walker, ill in bed, was visited by her local doctor, Sunderland – who, in addition to Mr Day, was treating her weak spine.

December

Saturday 1 At Lidgate in 25 minutes at 11 50/" - Miss Parkhill had disap-peared and staid away in the other room during my visit... *She thought I seemed indifferent yesterday* [about] *how the thing terminated between us whether she should be with me or not - I parried this very gallantly... I saw she got fidgety - said she could not keep Miss P- so long away. I said I would go in half-hour - however, seeing Miss W- uneasy, I jumped up & was off.* Mr Sunderland called before one - found Miss W- much better... [Mr Day] says her spine is <u>very</u> weak, & weakens her whole system - the seat of her complaint - should not take much exercise in a carriage or on horseback... talked like a quack, and as if nobody understood backs & spines like him – a vulgar, apparently uneducated man. In my walk at 2₁/₄... with John Booth holing & digging up about my rustic seat in the walk.

A letter arrived from Mr Ainsworth: *'another rigmarole - shall not answer it'*, commented Anne angrily. Why should she have to take responsibility for this problem as well?

---

[138] Presumably AW's promise of 'yes' to AL, ie promise to marry.

I have considered & re-considered
all you so kindly said to me on
Saturday in however painful and to
me to tell you, yet I must tell you
that as my convictions with regard to
its being wrong & against my duty remain,
I think we had better not meet again
till I have seen my sister's letter, for
my wretchedness only brings misery
upon you — & misery seems to increase
every day — I know not what to do for
the best —

Monday Decr 24th 1832.

Letter, Ann Walker to Anne Lister, 24 December 1832
SH:7/ML/644/1

7 NEXT TENANT OF MY HEART
2-31 December

Wednesday 5 Came in at 1 - found note from Miss Walker begging me to go as early as I could in the afternoon - her visitors to leave her at 4 to drink tea at Cliff-hill … Found also parcel from the nursery at Leamington (Cullis & co) sent by M-'s order: 6 Cercis Siliquastrum (arbor Judae or Judas trees) & 6 evergreen Luccomb oaks, & 1/2 gallon of Spanish chestnut, ditto mossy cup acorn, ditto quercus pedunculatus[139] - very nicely packed in straw - took John Booth & had the trees planted immediately…

Set off to Lidgate at 41/4 - rain - turned back & waited in the hut till the shower was over, & at Lidgate at 5 - dinner (mutton steak) a little before 6, tea at 6 - cosy evening - said how much I enjoyed our quiet tête-à-tête & was in very good spirits. Miss Parkhill & Miss & Miss Emily Rawson of Millhouse returned about 9.[140] [I] merely civil to Miss P-, kind & attentive to the 2 Misses R-, said my visit must be taken as partly to them. Miss W- read prayers - rainy evening so had determined to stay all night - went upstairs at 10 1/2.

Ann Walker possessed a strong religious sense of wickedness. 'Wrong' was a word that had very powerful meanings for her. Was this triggered partly because she had just heard back from her very respectably-married elder sister, Elizabeth Sutherland in Scotland?

Thursday 6 *Talking last night till two - said she should not suffer* [physically?] *for me - so declared I would not grubble her - she excited as she lay on me & I pretended great difficulty in keeping my word - I felt her over her chemise & this all but did the job for her. She owned she could not help it & that now she had got into the way of it… thought she should be getting wrong with somebody when I went away. 'Oh', thought I, 'this is plain enough'. Yet still she talked of her sufferings because she thought it*

---

[139] Judas tree: rosy-lilac flowers in May. *Quercus pedunculatus*: weeping English or Common Oak.

[140] Daughters of William Henry & Mary Rawson; Mary, sister of William Priestley, was AW's cousin.

wrong to have this connection with me. We argued this point - she will have it [that] she shall never marry, if not Mr Ainsworth. (Told her of the letter I had from him on Monday.) But she is quite man-keen, & the wrong with me is that I am not enough for her...

She will not do for me - I will not give her an opportunity of saying 'No' on the first of January. Miss W- read me last night the passage from her sister's letter respecting me - very sensible - advised Miss W-'s going abroad with me - thought it would do her good & be a great advantage to her, all my acquaintances being of a higher order. Yet all this did not seem to have much influence - she will not go abroad, & <u>now</u> will <u>not</u> leave Lidgate on my going away...

Off this morning at 9 55/" as soon as [I] dressed, without seeing any of the visitors - took my leave last night, not choosing to be more in contact with Miss P- than necessary...

Breakfast with my aunt - out at 11₃/₄ - with Pickles & his son John stubbing & getting up & planting thorns & hazels.

Anne Lister possessed a religious certainty that her relationship with Ann Walker was indeed sanctioned by God. She now decided to assert her authority even further over Ann by manipulating her guilt about the Reverend Ainsworth and her respect for her sister's opinion. She also tried to peel Ann away from her troublesome female companions.

Friday 7 With John Booth planting 2 or 3 thorns in the walk till 1 - then in 1/2 hour at Lidgate. Took Miss W- the form of prayers I sent from London for, & got bound at Whitleys, in crimson morocco with purple watered-silk fly-leaves & gilt edges - had written in it... at the beginning... 'Matthew vii 21', & ...at the end...A.L." [141] Gave her this - *& desired to have given into my charge (sealed up) all she had of Mr Ainsworth's letters... My decisions were not like hers - I did not say one thing today & another tomorrow... I had decided for her & was determined. She said 'No, no, she could not go abroad, it could not be so'. I said I was determined & should not attend to any 'No, no'. She burst into tears... I surely did not mean to take her abroad - said I should not exactly say what I intended - but now that I knew her sister to be a well-judging person, I*

[141] 'Not every one that saith unto me, Lord, Lord, shall enter into the kingdom of heaven; but he that doeth the will of my Father which is in Heaven.'

should do nothing that she would not approve. Miss W- said she had written to her. 'Well, then'said I, '& I shall write too. ''What, to tell about Mr Ainsworth?' 'No', said I, 'I have not thought of that, but I shall do what is necessary.' At the close of all this, she really seemed better - perhaps this present plan will answer best.

Miss Parkhill was in the room on my going in - spoke or rather bowed to her formally - and on my going out to point out where the cercis siliquastrum (Judas tree) I had brought her should be planted, Miss P- left the room. She goes on Monday & Miss Lydia Wilkinson then comes to Lidgate, of which I said I should be glad... Set off home...

1/2 hour talking to my aunt... Miss W- was not fit to be left at Lidgate... Dinner at 6 - afterwards wrote the whole of the above of today. *Will take Miss W- to York as soon after the rent day as I can... Perhaps this will do the girl good... at any rate I shall keep my power over her for the present at least.* John planted all the 350 hollies this afternoon.

As Anne Lister laid her plans, the 1832 election contest in Halifax began to accelerate.[142]

Saturday 8 At Lidgate at 10 - sat with Miss W- tête-à-tête in the dining room till 12 & then off back again to my walk. *Talked to Miss W- of going to York third or fourth of next month for three weeks or a month - to take plate & linen & have a good handsome lodging - & to call James by his sirname [sic], & make him powder - & have Joseph Booth under him – Sarah to be cook-housekeeper & Eugénie to meet us. A very nice plan, as she seemed to think. I laughed & said, 'Well, & after that, Leamington & then the south.' 'Yes', said she, '& then you mean abroad - but I will not go' - and then she got into the old story of [how] she felt she was not doing right morally, could not consent, had determined to say 'No'. I laughed it all off at the moment. She grieved over behaving so ill on Wednesday night, that is, being lovingly-inclined - yet let me grubble her this morning gladly enough.*

Said to myself as I left her, 'What a goose she is - but I will not care for that or her sorrow'. I said I would sleep there on Monday. With Pickles & his son planting hazels & with John Booth digging up near the rustic chair all the afternoon till 5 - then came home & paid P- up to tonight.

---

[142] Parliament was dissolved on 3 Dec; in Halifax, Tuesday 11 was fixed for nomination & 12-3 for polling. See John Lister (ed.), 'Some Extracts from the Diary of a Halifax Lady', *Halifax Guardian* (1887-92), LXXXII.

Dressed - dinner at 6 - read over Mr Wortley's 2 long speeches in the Halifax Guardian (no. 2 of the new Tory paper) – wrote… to the Honorable Lady Stuart… '[I] almost despaired of going very far on the continent just now, things in such a state of uncertainty & confusion' - she knew how sincerely Mr Wortley had my good wishes - should be glad to make his acquaintance some time, when it might be in my power to shew him some attention… Sure of his election - our cause drooping & many giving up for lost, till Mr W-'s eloquence & admirable management won it back - his 2 last speeches had fired all his old friends & gained him many new ones. Sent her (Lady S-) this morning's H-x paper for her to judge for herself…. Rainy, drizzling day, but excellent for planting.

Despite her female companions, shy and isolated Ann Walker was left vulnerable without an effective protector. What would life hold if Anne Lister left her?

Tuesday 11 *Without any persuasion she came to me at once last night – and, forgetting all the wrong, she lay in my arms all the night - and had three good long grubblings, nothing loth… We awoke at seven and talked till eight - now that she sees me inclined to be off, she wants to be on again, said no more about the wrong, but began to think she was throwing away her happiness & said she could not bear to part with me… I left her immediately afterwards without shewing any of my usual reluctance to go.*

I was dressed in an hour… Downstairs at 9½ - Miss W- read prayers – breakfast – a little while tête-à-tête with Miss Wilkinson – very civil to her – then at 10 40/" proposed Miss W-'s going out & our all going at the same time. *Went to my room for my hat – & Miss W- came to me & staid about an hour - evidently courting me more as I court her less… I kept to my gravity – told her of her inconsistency & indecision, & asked gently how I could possibly trust her? But still professed my earnest wish to do anything in the world to serve her, & behaved most handsomely - thinking to myself, 'Well, what should I do with her? Be off – & have no more to say to her.' I shall keep up this gravity.* All went out together at 11 & parted at the William Priestleys' door…

[Talking] to my aunt - *told her that I knew not how things were, for now again that I wanted to be off, Miss W- seemed fretting to bring it on again, but I should think & care nothing about it.*

Meanwhile, Anne Lister was approached by the 'blues' about one of her enfranchised tenants living within the Halifax borough.

Note from Mr Parker [family lawyer] from Mr Wortley's committee room begging me to make sure of John Bottomley's vote. Out with John at 2 - finished digging up what I yesterday (or the day before) christened John's garden[143] - just under the Calf Croft thorn clump, & moved 2 rhododendrons [144] there from the east slope... Came in at 5 - about 1/2 hour with my aunt - dressed - dined at 6 - read the first 60 pages of Monteath's Forester's Guide, which came this morning from Whitley's.

Had John Bottomley, having sent for him to tell him to vote for Wortley tomorrow - had 1/4 hour's talk - he promised to vote for him... They [the Whigs] had all been at him, & some said they would not employ him again if he would not vote their way, but he told them how I wanted him to vote - and seeming to care nothing about it but that he thought he ought to oblige me. It is quite useless to leave such men as he uninfluenced - he knows nothing & cares nothing about it, & is likely best satisfied with the idea of pleasing somebody he knows.... John says the shew of hands today [in the Piece Hall] was ten to one in favour of Stocks & Briggs.[145] Read over the Courier.

Of the newly-enfranchised voters in new boroughs like Halifax, small-scale tenants like Bottomley were vulnerable to coercion. Some men, like Throp, had no vote yet.

Wednesday 12 Had Throp - if I could get him his shop window made & new roof raised a couple of feet, [he] would vote as I liked all his life - has no vote this time because his landladies pay the taxes - has about 5 D.W. & pays £70 a year for the land & buildings (the latter poor enough)....[146] Throp brought 200 good ones [hollies] this

---

[143] Possibly the 'Garden end Field' marked on the 1791 map, cultivated by gardener/manservant John.

[144] Introduced earlier; species from the Himalayas were coming in from the 1820s

[145] At this nomination meeting, Wortley was nominated by Christopher Rawson and seconded by John Waterhouse. Stocks spoke in favour of ending both the slave trade and children under 12 working in factories; after the show of hands, Wood & Wortley demanded a poll; Lister, 'Some Extracts', LXXXII.

[146] Neither Throp nor AL really yet understood electoral qualifications in detail, as it was all so new. D.W is an abbreviation of Day's Work (about two-thirds of an acre).

morning & 40 box....

Wrote... to I. N- to thank her for the brace of pheasants which arrived from her to me yesterday - told her the state of the poll on closing tonight (began this morning): Wood 180, Briggs 176, Stocks 128, Wortley 120 - but hope of Wortley's gaining ground tomorrow. Hoped to be off from here before the end of next month...

Dinner at 6 1/2... Went into the other room at 9 50/" - 1/4 hour talking to Marian about the estate - she said my uncle's will was a very foolish one etc etc. She had got a copy of it from Mr Parker - I made no remark on this - odd enough - she knew the probate copy was in the house & she might have copied it whenever she liked, had she asked me for it... All this passed before my aunt - I take these things pretty coolly nowadays.

Ann Walker's cousin was naturally among those active locally in securing 'blue' votes.

Thursday 13 Mr Henry Edwards junior of Pye-nest called for a few minutes about John Bottomley's vote - gave him a note as follows: 'John Bottomley, I hear mistakes are made by voters going to the wrong booth - I send this by Mr Henry Edwards of Pye-nest, & wish you would go with him'... Begged Mr H. E- to shew the man this & then tear it up...

Out at 10 - found Pickles just come up from the hedge stubbing between Calf croft & round Ing etc - had him down holing near the hut....

At Lidgate at 3 3/4. *Miss W- very glad & much affected at seeing me - she thought it all at [an] end between us & was overcome - gradually consoled, & [I] said that if she really could not bear to part with me & could [not] decidedly make up her mind, I would do all I could & reverse my intention even at the eleventh hour.* Miss W- wished me to stay all night to look over the administrative accounts... Dinner at 6 - tea at 6 1/2 - at the accounts (Miss W- left me at 10 to read prayers to the servants) till 11 20/".

Friday 14 *Talking & pressing & love-making till after three this morning... She lay upon me & in my arms - then slept to near eight & then talked till after ten. [I] insinuated, first time, that our present intercourse, without any tie between us, must be as wrong as any other transient connection. She seems to think refusing me is refusing her best chance of happiness & is more* *likely than ever to accept me?* Breakfast at 11 - at the accounts again & talking till out at 1 20/" - then walked together to the hut in my walk - sat there near an hour till John came down after his dinner. Miss W- planted the mulberrry tree (that came yesterday) & the <u>magnolia grandiflora</u> that came this morning with 80 more box, 10 yews etc.

Walked back in about 25 minutes & left her at her own door at 4 - then returned to my walk... *Miss W- told me in the hut if she said 'Yes' again, it should be binding - it should be the same as marriage & she would give me no cause to be jealous - made no objection to what I proposed, that is, her declaring it on the Bible & taking the sacrament with me at Shibden or Lightcliffe church. She may do as she likes - but we now seem quite as likely as ever to get together? Am I foolish to risk it again?*

What is absolutely beyond doubt is the seriousness with which Anne viewed the intimacy. It must not be 'transient', and that meant that their proposed marriage should be formally sanctified in an Anglican church with appropriate ritual.[147]

Meanwhile the election result was announced: Wood (235) and Briggs (242) were elected, Stocks received 186 votes, and Wortley came last with 174.[148] Losing to the Whigs was a deep political disappointment for Anne and her friends. Stoically, she recorded no lamentation in her diary, merely sending Lady Stuart Saturday's *Halifax Guardian.* [149]

Saturday 15 Out at 11 5/", at Lidgate in 25 minutes - Mr Day came almost immediately &, on seeing Miss W-'s back, said it was as much better... to go on rubbing as before - Humbug! I very civil to him, shook hands & half-persuaded him to vote for Wortley (instead of Briggs) another time....

Miss W-... *had begun the copy of a letter to her sister - to ask her opinion &*

---

[147] Possibly what AL had in mind was marriage by licence, which (with no banns called) gave privacy to élite couples.

[148] *Halifax Borough Election, The Poll Book*, Halifax 1833, p 16; the figures AL gives are slightly different. Bottomley had voted for Wortley,

[149] AL also wrote to VC, 31.12.1832, despairingly of politics, unions, & how sick she was of public events.

advice about living with me - if her sister approves she will do it - & it is to be as a marriage between us. (She kept to this, even after the letter came from Miss Bentley with a melancholy account of Mr Ainsworth... All a very unfair intruding of himself upon her remembrance...) She was melancholy for about an hour but then recovered her spirits amazingly - sat on my knee... Reconciled to go abroad & [as] if our being together was all but certain - depending only [on] her sister - the letter to go next Tuesday.

Meanwhile, Anne wrote a long and somewhat disingenuous letter about her travel plans and attachment to Shibden to Mariana Lawton - who was helping her find a manservant:

Sunday 16 'No objection to give £20 wages if that is to include washing - give clothes such & so many as I think proper - he would have all housework to attend to,[150] & be a good deal about me - his being able to read and write indispensable... Yet the thought of exile from poor Shibden always makes me melancholy - come what may, I have been happier here than anywhere else... Providence orders all things wisely... I am attached to my own people - they are accustomed to my oddities, are kind, are <u>civilized</u> to me...[151] A great deal will, & must, depend on that someone, known or unknown, whom I still hope for as the comfort of my evening hour.... Must go & live on bread & water - whether I shall do so or not, is doubtful - busy just now among my young trees, pruning.'

Monday 17 *Incurred a cross last night thinking of Miss W-.... Miss W- not quite so well today - had been miserable again about Mr Ainsworth. She read me... what she meant to write to her sister - asking her opinion & advice on the subject of my proposal to our living together - she seemed wavering, & I said the thing seemed now as uncertain between us as ever I talked a little sentiment & argued against Mr A-, & pressed her hard to decide - & one while [ie on one occasion] proposed not seeing her again till Christmas Day, when she expected her sister's answer. Then I brought her round to say... that if her sister approved, there would no longer be any obstacle between [us] & she would say a positive & decisive 'Yes'. She had another letter from her [sister] evidently regretting that she had given up the thought of going abroad with me - &, as far as Mrs Sutherland well could, advising*

---

[150] Illegible: possibly horse-work or home-work

[151] Probably a reference to loyal tenantry and servants.

Miss W- to reconsider the thing...

Home in $1/2$ hour... Wrote the following to go tomorrow morning to Mr Jeremiah Rawson... 'Dear Sir - If I don't hear from you respecting the coal before the end of this week, I shall feel myself at liberty to dispose of it... I am, sir, etc A Lister'.

Anne was running out of patience with Ann Walker's dithering.

Wednesday 19 Began to rain - took shelter 10 minutes at Lower brea ... at Lidgate about $3_1/4$ ... Sat with Miss W- till about $5_1/4$ & home in $1/2$ hour... *Miss W- had been miserable again as usual.... I said I saw she would be no more able to decide even when the answer [from her sister] came than now. My manner shewed that I was not quite pleased - I said the additional length of unnecessary suspence was not fair - had she known half the uneasiness she gave, I was sure she could not have found in her heart to act as she did.*

She sobbed & cried & said I made her very nervous... I expressed my great sorrow at this... I made two or three moves to leave her but she hung on me & kept me & said she was better after a glass of sherry... She did not know what would become of her when I was gone - if she could but hope to see me again... I said I confidently anticipated her sister's answer, if she (Miss W-) had written what she told me [she] would...

How can such a girl make me happy? I said to myself, 'If I really cared much all this would make me miserable'... Surely the thing is virtually at an end now?...

Dinner at $6_1/4$ - could not settle to do anything - sat leaning, & sleeping on the sofa till my mind was composed. Went into the other room at $9_3/4$ & staid talking to my aunt till $10_1/2$ - told her of Mr [Jeremiah] R-'s note (tho' had not named it to the rest) - & said how things were with Miss W-, she would either marry in a twelve-month, no good match, or go to the dogs - that is, be poorly & unhappy & perhaps, like many such nervous people, take more than she ought (drink) at last - she had everything to be wished for but the power of enjoying it.

Amid the normal business of coal leases, visiting the Priestleys and religious duties, Anne Lister still felt deeply unsettled – and uncharacteristically lethargic.

Thursday 20 Mr Musgrave (our vicar) came... & staid, administering the sacrament to my aunt, Hemingway, Cordingley & myself, &

talking till 2₁/4 - mentioned how many objects of charity there were in H-x &c, & my aunt & I therefore gave him a sovereign each to be distributed as he thought best....

At Lightcliffe at 3 40/" at Mr William Priestley's... Then, not choosing to pass Miss Walker's door without calling, went in for 25 minutes to inquire after her - she said it was very good of me to call on her today. *We might have had a scene but my calm dignity of manner kept it off - she consulted me about one or two things... She will most likely be miserable again tonight - & my going to her will keep me in her mind.*

Saturday 22 *She harped on Cliff-hill & Mr Ainsworth – I argued as usual... She wants my services & time & friendship & to keep her money to herself. Will even Mr A- be able to get* [hold] *her fast? I left her with less care than ever... I may use her person* [body] *freely enough.*

Helped by her coal agent James Holt, the haggling with the Rawsons was at last coming to a conclusion.

Monday 24. Very fine morning – ground whitish with frost F48₁/2° at 8 10/" am – *incurred a cross just before getting up, thinking of Miss W- exactly as if she had been my regular mistress – respect for her is quite gone in those matters at least... Mused (first time) on sending her anonymously from Bradford or London Ovid's* Art of Love.

Mr Jeremiah Rawson came at 9 5/" – kept him waiting 10 minutes, & went down at 9₁/4, & had him 1/4 hour or 20 minutes - had the coal plan... I said 10 acres should be stated in the agreement... Mr R- said Holt had [said] the coal was not worth more than £160 per acre... *Mr R- said he was never beaten but by ladies & I had beaten him.* [I] *said gravely, 'It is the intellectual part of us that makes a bargain, & that has no sex or ought* [to] *have none'.* 152

Tuesday 25 Xmas day – very stormy... too rainy for Miss W- to go to church, & sat with her till 1... *Grubbled her a little... She said she did not think it right – wished we could do without it. At breakfast I referred to her scruples & wishes - & said I would try not to care for her in that particular way... Sat talking all morning – combatting her scruples - & really thought I had made some impression & done her good, till, on going away & asking*

---

152 Also on Monday, letter from AW: SH:7/ML/644/1, 24.12.1832, 'My convictions with regard to its being wrong & against my duty remain... My wretchedness only brings misery upon you.'

her to write & tell me how she was tomorrow, she said, 'Oh, no, she should be no better', & burst into tears. And I left her thinking, 'I never saw such a hopeless person in my life – how miserable' - said I to myself, 'thank God my own mind's not like hers – what could I do with her?'

Walked... by Lower brea into my walk – at the hut at 1 35/" – knelt down & prayed & thanked God as well as I could for ten minutes then sat down in the hut & tried to sleep – musing & slumbering about ? hour – then sauntered in my walk.

Wednesday 26 Off from the hut to Lidgate... *Her scruples seem abated... Talked of keeping on Lidgate for us to return to – her going to York & Langton [the Norcliffes] & our being off on the last day of next month... But I attached in reality no importance to all this, well knowing that tomorrow she might be all on the other side of the question.* Home at 6½.

Thursday 27 Down the fields to my walk – the great hazel removed yesterday to the bottom of Calf Croft.

At last, the long-awaited reply from Elizabeth Sutherland arrived.

Saturday 29 Wrote out part of coal-lease instructions, and at 8½ [received] note... from Miss Walker – *'I have had a letter from my sister, saying everything that is kind... She advises our taking lodgings in York for the winter – going to visit her in the summer – then, if we are both in the same mind, make our tour of the continent next year - she adds that she believes I think at this present time that I shall never marry...'[153]*

Went on with writing out coal-lease instructions then at 9 50/" went into the other room & staid talking to my aunt till came to my room at 10 40/"... Well, surely it is settled now & she will waver no more – I will be off as soon as I can – how little Mrs Sutherland guesses the real truth - & how coolly she plans for us – her plans would never do for me – have all the pother for nothing – merely to take care of her till Mr Ainsworth was ready for her – I am not quite so simple as that.

Anne Lister was still living the incessant tensions: she was pleased to be 'off' travelling with Ann Walker, but she remained jaundiced about the pull of conventional marriage for such women. The last day of the year offered an opportunity for reflection.

---

[153] SH:7/ML/646/1, 29.12.1832.

Monday 31 *Our going to York apparently at an end – parted in tears, both of us, I saying I never did or could understand her...* Dinner at 6¼ - afterward asleep on the sofa till 9 – *awoke, better – this girl, without really having my esteem or affection, somehow or other unhinges me whenever I see her...* Well! Here is the end of another year! How different this new year's eve from the last! *tho' in each case, unsuccessful love-making* – what will be the leading event of the next 12 months... ?

How different my situation now & this time last year – quite off with M-, Vere married & off at Rome, but we are, & are likely to be, excellent friends. Miss W-, as it were, come & gone, known & forgotten - & myself, what I have never been before since [the age of] *fifteen - absolutely untied to anyone. I never stood so alone - & yet I am far happier than... I have been of long - I am used & reconciled to my loneness - I shall do, some way or other, what*[ever] *adventure will come next. Who will be the next tenant of my heart? Providence orders all things wisely.*

Afterword: 1833

After December 1832, Anne Lister's interest in landscaping Shibden was overtaken by her desire to exploit the estate's mining potential, and she developed a competitive coal strategy.[154] However, she retained her ambitions to improve Shibden architecturally and from 1836 began to put some of her grand plans into effect – giving us the house we now know today.

Meanwhile, what happened to Anne's plans for settling and travelling with Ann Walker? In spring 1833 Ann was whisked away northward to Scotland to stay with Elizabeth Sutherland and her family - and to consult doctors in Inverness. However, Thomas Ainsworth continued to pursue her, pressing his suit and proposing marriage – which Ann rejected.

---

[154] Her study of geology necessarily became very practical.
Meanwhile, the *Beagle* returned in 1836, and Darwin able to break the intellectual deadlock between the uniformitarians and the catastophists.

From June 1833 Anne Lister herself also set off, leaving responsibility for the estate with her new steward Samuel Washington. She travelled southwards, staying with Mariana Lawton, and in London seeing Lady Stuart de Rothesay and Lady Stuart, plus Lady Vere Cameron and her new baby. With her two new servants, Thomas and Eugénie, she travelled first to Paris, and then stayed in Copenhagen - where she was presented at the Danish court.

So did Anne and Ann come together again? Who in reality was *'the next tenant of my heart'*? Readers wanting to follow this story may like to turn to the sequel, *Female Fortune: the Anne Lister diaries 1833-36.*

Note on the Text

Why late 1832 - again?

As indicated earlier, I originally worked on the late 1832 diary for *Presenting the Past* (1994), and returned to this again to undertake further transcription for the introductory chapters of *Female Fortune: the Anne Lister diaries 1833-36* (1998). But recently wider public interest in Anne persuaded me that, with only a few short passages published so far, a fuller transcription, setting these few well-known passages in context, was now urgently required.

The entire diaries (1806-40) run to no fewer than four million words - within which the late 1832 journal (volume 15) presents a particularly richly-packed few months.[155] Yet of these months, the well-known passages were limited essentially to just the 1832 election and a few coded passages – with little connection between them.[156] The rest of this diary remained lost in a dense mist of Anne's daily toing-and-froing on the estate. For what fills these pages (to the intense dismay of researchers stumbling upon them) is Anne's active and detailed engagement with Shibden's landscape. Indeed, twelve years ago, I too was dismissive, and wrote loftily that 'the barrowing, channelling and culverting details are tedious to all but a landscape historian collecting data'.[157] Not so. I now realise that the connections between landscape and desire are crucial.

Criteria for selection

---

[155] Volume 15, covering 12.5 months, is almost a quarter of a million words long; AL wrote roughly 640 words each day in her diary at this point.

[156] For the 1832 election, *PtP* p. 39-40, and *FF* p. 46-8; for the courtship and seduction, *PtP* p. 40-4, and *FF* p. 59—70

[157] *PtP*, p 44

Guided by the signposts provided by earlier editors,[158] I therefore plunged into 1832 for a third time. I identified the eight-and-a-half month period (from mid-April to New Year's Eve) of the diary, totalling roughly 170,000 words.[159] From this, I have selected about 25,000 words to present here (ie about 15 per cent of the original diary). In comparison with other editions, it intentionally offers a small but richer slice of the Anne Lister cake.[160]

The criteria for inclusion and omission are largely similar to those of *Female Fortune*. First, I have aimed to present a coherent narrative thread, focusing on the three key themes (love, landscape, politics) and the key relationships flowing from these. Second, I wanted to allow the reader to enter Anne Lister's own world - for her world was by no means our world. I have therefore tried to reflect the stupendous breadth of her activities (eg her wide reading at the cutting-edge of science), and to retain some of the seemingly breathtaking juxtapositions (for instance, seduction and rent-rolls) that jump out at the twenty-first century reader. I have retained some of the texture of daily life, while paring down the central narrative so that it is easier to follow.

Third, of the diaries as a whole, about one-sixth was written in code. For these 1832 months the code rises probably to at least one-third; and I have retained roughly that proportion – the better able to reflect the connections between public and private, between landscape and desire. The material that has been omitted records mainly tediously repetitive description: daily weather and temperature measurement; daily meals and how many minutes each took; extended summaries of countless letters. I have also omitted much of the arcane detail of her estate work; for, as I wrote

---

[158] Notably John Lister (1887-92) and Phyllis Ramsden (1958-85); see *PtP* p. 12-22.

[159] 170,000 words is nearly one-twentieth of the complete diaries, 125,000 about a thirtieth

[160] This compares to JL, 5% of whole diaries; HW (*I Know*) 13% of 1817-24 diaries; FF 10% of 1833-36 diaries; and NOF 1.5% of whole diaries.

seven years ago, Anne obsessively and relentlessly recorded 'every tree planted... every boulder moved'.[161]

Editorial conventions

As in *Female Fortune*, excisions are indicated by ellipses.[162] To ensure clarity and accessibility, most of Anne's habitual abbreviations have been extended; the exceptions are those few familiar names (eg Miss W- for Ann Walker) listed on the page showing Anne Lister's Abbreviations. Anne's informal diary-style punctuation, using frequent dashes, has broadly been retained; however, to aid readability some punctuation has been added, with major shifts in subject matter indicated by a new sentence or paragraph.

Square brackets have been used only sparingly, usually to indicate when a word or phrase has been added where meaning would otherwise be unclear.[163] Endnotes have also been kept to a minimum, used to suggest possible meanings or to provide necessary contextual information. In other words, explanatory scholarly apparatus has been kept to a minimum here. But to retain a sense of distance from Anne Lister's world, I have retained her spellings (eg shew, staid), and her own conventions for recording time.

The origin and status of sections of text are indicated by distinct typefaces: coded passage are printed in *italics*, and editorial linking passages in a larger typeface and not indented. I had intended my linking passages to be minimal, but comment from readers urged me to provide more edi-torial guidance, and this I have done.

---

[161] *FF*, p 77.

[162] Except at the start or end of each daily entry; major omissions are noted in endnotes.

[163] They have not been used where Anne made an unintended (but understandable) slip in either hand-written or coded passages (eg an omitted or duplicated letter or word)

Finally I have, of course, retained Anne's day-by-day chronology, but have presented the material as seven broad chronological sections, to reflect the crucial connections between the key themes, and the organic nature of her being, her life: here, landscape and desire are intertwined.

Abbreviations

AL	Anne Lister
AL, date	Anne Lister diaries
AW	Ann Walker
FF	*Female Fortune...*
I Know	*I Know my own Heart...*
PtP	*Presenting the Past...*
SH	Shibden Hall

Full book titles are given below

SELECT REFERENCES

PRIMARY SOURCES

SH:2/M/1/2/2	A Map of Shibden Hall Estate belonging to Mr James Lister, 1791
SH:3/L/92	Catalogue of the Valuable Library of Books, Maps etc (formerly the property of the late Mrs Lister of Shibden Hall) to be sold at auction..., 1846
SH:7/ML	Anne Lister correspondence
SH:7/ML/E/15	Anne Lister journal (volume 15) 1 Jan 1831 – 12 Jan 1833

OTHER MATERIAL

Lister John (ed), 'Some Extracts from the Diary of a Halifax Lady', *Halifax Guardian* (1887-92)

Halifax Borough Election, The Poll Book, Halifax 1833

BOOKS - GENERAL

Foreman, Amanda, *Georgiana: Duchess of Devonshire*, Harper Collins, 1998
Gribbin, John, *Science: a history 1543-2001*, Allen Lane, 2002
MacDougall, Elizabeth (ed.), *John Claudius Loudon and the Early Nineteenth Century in Great Britain*, Dumbarton Oaks, 1980
Perkin, Joan, *Women and Marriage in Nineteenth-Century England*, Routledge, 1989
Sheeran, George, *Landscape Gardens in West Yorkshire 1680-1880*, Wakefield Historical Publications, 1990
Vickery, Amanda, *The Gentleman's Daughter: Women's Lives in Georgian England*, Yale University Press, 1998

BOOKS, ARTICLES AND THESES – ANNE LISTER

Liddington, Jill, *Presenting the Past: Anne Lister of Halifax 1791-1840*, Pennine Pens, 1994, 2010
Liddington, Jill, *Female Fortune: land, gender and authority: the Anne Lister diaries and other writings 1833-36*, Rivers Oram Press, 1998
Salter, Polly, *The Scientific Life of a Genteel Yorkshire Woman*, University of Leeds (unpublished essay), 2000
Westwood, Rosalind & Brown, Pete, *Shibden Hall, Halifax: a visitor's guide*, Calderdale Leisure Services, 1998
Whitbread, Helena, *I Know my own heart: the diaries of Anne Lister 1791-1840* [1817-24], Virago Press, 1988.
Whitbread, Helena, *No Priest but Love: the journals of Anne Lister from 1824-1826*, Smith Settle, 1992. Reissued with new title, 2010
Since *Nature's Domain* was first published in 2003, public interest in Anne Lister has grown - along with a number of new books:
Steidele, Angela, *Gentleman Jack: Regency Landowner, Seducer & Secret Diarist*, Serpent's Tail, 2018. (This biography, translated from German, relies heavily on the work of Helena Whitbread and myself.)
Calderdale Council (Angela Clare), *Anne Lister of Shibden Hall*, Calderdale Museums, 2018. A sumptuously illustrated booklet.
Bray, Alan, *The Friend*, University of Chicago Press, 2003. (A scholarly placing of Anne Lister in her traditionalist world.)
Euler, Cat, *Moving Between Worlds: Gender, Class, Politics, Sexuality & Women's Networks*, York University PhD, 1995. (This authoritative analysis of Anne Lister & her worlds is now available on-line.)

Index

Other Books by Jill Liddington

One Hand Tied Behind Us: the rise of the women's suffrage movement (with Jill Norris) Virago Press, 1978, 1984, 2000

The Life and Times of a Respectable Rebel: Selina Cooper 1864-1946 Virago Press, 1984

The Long Road to Greenham: feminism and anti-militarism in Britain since 1820. Virago Press, 1989

Presenting the Past: Anne Lister of Halifax 1791-1840 Pennine Pens, 1994, 2010

Female Fortune: Land, Gender & Authority: The Anne Lister Diaries 1833-36, Rivers Oram Press, 1998

Rebel Girls, Virago Press, 2006
Vanishing for the Vote, MUP, 2014

More details of Pennine Pens
publications and web design at

www.penninepens.co.uk